How To Books

Becoming a
Complementary Therapist

Becoming a Complementary Therapist

How to start a career in the new caring professions

LINDA WILSON
2nd edition

How To Books

Published by How To Books Ltd,
3 Newtec Place, Magdalen Road,
Oxford OX4 1RE, United Kingdom.
Tel: (01865) 793806. Fax: (01865) 248780.
email: info@howtobooks.co.uk
http://www.howtobooks.co.uk

First edition 1998
Second edition 2000

British Library Cataloguing in Publication Data
A catalogue record for this book is available from
the British Library

Cover design by Shireen Nathoo Design
Cover image PhotoDisc

Produced for How To Books by Deer Park Productions
Typeset by PDQ Typesetting, Newcastle-under-Lyme
Printed and bound by The Cromwell Press, Trowbridge,
Wiltshire

Contents

List of Illustrations

Foreword

Although its guiding principles are ancient, complementary therapy is a relatively young discipline within modern healthcare. Linda Wilson has clearly explained the role of complementary therapy and accurately described the path towards professional commitment.

In certain cultures, particularly those of the Far East, medical treatment has traditionally been regarded as a complementary arrangement. Quality of care is balanced with striving for cure, and the collaborative nature of treatment – the relationship between client and therapist – has always been stressed.

We have seen in recent years that complementary therapies are increasingly attracting the interest of established medical professionals, who find its influence a balance to the formality of their existing roles. Linda has observed, however, that many seeking professional training in the therapies are people looking for a change in career or personal direction; they may or may not have a clinical background but they hold an inner conviction that the ethos of complementary therapy is 'right'. Her advice to them is practical and encouraging, as well as inspiring.

The reasons why someone might choose to have complementary therapy are also usually much more personal than with conventional treatment. The therapies involve direct physical contact and are designed to facilitate the emotional expression of the client. Consequently the personal qualities of the practitioner are significant. Linda has rightly emphasised this, together with the implications and fulfilling opportunities presented by a career in complementary therapies.

Linda's experience as a therapist and trainer enables her to describe precisely and reassuringly the route to a successful career. Her book is well researched and meets a real need for information and guidance. I am sure it will be widely read and I welcome it as an important contribution towards the wider availability of complementary practice.

Stewart Mitchell
Director, The School of Complementary Therapies,
Exeter UK

Preface
to the Second Edition

Complementary medicine continues to go from strength to strength. Rarely a week goes by without positive media coverage of the effectiveness of therapies. Some medical schools now include complementary medicine modules in their curriculum in order to give trainee doctors an awareness of the principles and practice of the major therapies. University teaching of complementary therapies is expanding rapidly. The Appendix contains details of university degree and postgraduate courses which might interest the qualified therapist wishing to acquire an academic foundation for practice, as well as the more academic student wishing to enter complementary medicine. Some of the schools of acupuncture, herbal medicine, homeopathy, and osteopathy listed in Useful Addresses now offer degrees validated by universities.

This new edition will help people who are starting out in complementary medicine, or thinking of doing so. I hope qualified therapists and healthcare professionals will find inspiration for additional training. Several more therapies are included in this new edition and some, such as craniosacral therapy, iridology and zero balancing, are designed as postgraduate training for those who already have qualifications in orthodox or complementary medicine. Descriptions of the therapies are necessarily brief. I have attempted to give a succinct overview of typical course content for each therapy. Please bear in mind that course content and terminology varies from school to school. The resource section has been enlarged and updated with email and web sites to help the reader access more detailed information quickly and easily.

Whilst knowledge and accreditation are of great importance, we must remember that complementary medicine is where science and spirituality meet. Some of the most effective therapists have few academic qualifications, but possess healing abilities which cannot be examined and graded.

Linda Wilson

Acknowledgements

I would like to thank Dorothy Stephens for sparking off the idea of writing this book, and for her encouragement along the way. I am grateful to all the training schools and universities for the information they so willingly provided about their courses. Many of my friends and colleagues have provided advice and inspiration. I would particularly like to thank Jo Hogan, Andrew Luty, Sue and Simon Lilly, Lillian Stoltenberg, Guy Mitchell and Sue Harris.

Lucy Grant STAT read the manuscript and made valuable comments. Lucy ran the Longbrook Centre in Exeter with enormous energy and dedication for ten years and has been a source of inspiration for me and many other practitioners.

I would like to thank editor Nikki Read for her patience and encouragement and Cheryl Thornburg for her artwork. Finally, I would like to thank Paul Edwards for unstintingly providing both technical and moral support.

Acknowledgements for the second edition
I am very grateful to Mark Totterdell for his assistance with research and editing. I would like to thank Duncan Hulin, Sue Lilly, Zanna Heighton and Will Wilson for their help with the text, Jennifer Hooper for her helpful comments and constructive criticism, and Emma Short for her artwork.

1

Introducing Complementary Therapies

DEFINING 'COMPLEMENTARY'

There has been much discussion about the words 'alternative' and 'complementary'. '**Alternative**', strictly speaking, would apply to those therapies which offer a complete system of treatment without the patient visiting a doctor or other medical practitioner. '**Complementary**' would therefore apply to those therapies which can be used alongside conventional medical treatments. Some people prefer to get it absolutely right by referring to '**complementary and alternative medicine**'. This is commonly seen in official reports and tends to be abbreviated to CAM. In this book the word 'complementary' is used, reflecting the preference of most therapists.

A recent Scottish Office report, *Complementary Medicine and the National Health Service*, suggests that the term may be loosely defined as 'referring to treatment systems other than those employed in conventional (allopathic) medicine....In practice it refers to a wide range of health interventions originating from different cultures across thousands of years of history'. Many therapies are indeed based on ancient knowledge, e.g. traditional Chinese acupuncture, and are as effective and relevant as ever.

APPRECIATING THE BENEFITS

Why have complementary therapies become so popular over the past few years? The following are just a few of the many possible reasons:

- public dissatisfaction with side-effects of drug treatments and surgery
- frustration with long waiting times for NHS treatments
- desire to take more responsibility for own health care
- desire for freedom of choice and more involvement in decision making

- appreciation of personal attention from complementary therapists, with appointments lasting between 30 minutes and 2 hours

- appreciation of the holistic approach, which views the patient as a whole person and takes lifestyle and other factors into account.

There is a great need for balanced information about all forms of complementary medicine, both for the public and for health professionals. It has an important role to play in preventative health care and in cases where conventional medicine has no more to offer. As more and more people experience the benefits of various therapies, so more and more people are inspired to become therapists themselves.

AN EXPANDING FIELD

Complementary medicine is one of the fastest growing sectors of employment in the UK. In the USA and many European countries, state authorisation is required for practitioners of most therapies. This is not the case in the UK, which means that complementary medicine is free to grow and develop in response to public demand. This is a positive factor in terms of freedom of choice for the public, but there are negative aspects too, e.g. there is no obligation for all therapists to meet particular standards.

Researchers at the University of Exeter estimate that there could be as many as 45,000 complementary therapists working in the UK. They estimate that each practitioner would see around 80 individual patients a year, each patient being seen a number of times. This would suggest that more than 3 million patients consult a practitioner each year. Other researchers put the figure even higher, at around 4 million. It is possible that the total number of people ever treated by complementary practitioners could be as high as 20 per cent of the population.

Integrating conventional and complementary medicine

These figures indicate how the field is growing. Opportunities are plentiful for people who wish to build careers in complementary medicine. Whilst most therapists work in private practice, there are now many openings within the NHS. This has to expand because more and more doctors and nurses are training in various therapies. It is rare nowadays to find a reflexology or aromatherapy class without at least one qualified nurse amongst the students.

Complementary medicine is not yet an integral part of medical training in the UK, unlike in Germany, where medical students study herbal medicine too. However, some nursing courses do have a complementary health module which gives students an overview of the different therapies.

The Foundation for Integrated Medicine is a charity which was formed at the suggestion of the Prince of Wales in order to promote the integration of complementary and conventional medicine. The charity recently produced a report which estimated that as many as 750,000 complementary health consultations occur within the NHS each year, and that nearly 40 per cent of GP practices in England provide access to complementary health care for patients.

Two more reports, *Tomorrow's Doctors* by the General Medical Council and the BMA's *Complementary Medicine: New Approaches to Good Practice*, both acknowledge that complementary medicine may have a part to play within the NHS, delivering cost-effective treatment to patients.

So we see that complementary medicine is well on the way to becoming integrated into the mainstream of health-care provision in the UK. This is good news for anybody thinking of training as a therapist.

SETTING STANDARDS

The medical profession has well-defined standards and qualifications, which are clearly understood by those inside the profession and by the public. Doctors use the title 'Doctor' and the letters MB, BS after their name. They qualify after a demanding six-year training. Nurses too have letters after their name, e.g. RGN, RMN, and their training spans three years. The public understands and, usually, trusts the system. It is well established and inspires confidence.

The interests and views of the medical profession are represented by such bodies as the General Medical Council, the British Medical Association, The Royal College of Nursing, etc. These organisations are well-respected and are often quoted in the media.

Complementary medicine lacks such a clearly defined and organised structure. This is a serious disadvantage. It means that the medical profession, the public and potential students of complementary therapies have great difficulty in understanding the qualifications and standards within the industry.

Creating more clarity in complementary medicine

Anyone looking in the *Yellow Pages* for a hypnotherapist will find names followed by a variety of letters, e.g. CHyp, CMH, DHP, MNCH. What do they all mean? These letters indicate that the therapists trained at certain colleges and belong to certain professional associations, but how is anyone outside the hypnotherapy profession supposed to judge the competence of the therapist?

The Department of Health recognised that, if complementary medicine were to be included in future policy-making, information about the structure of the industry would be essential. The Centre for Complementary Health Studies at the University of Exeter was therefore commissioned to carry out a survey, which was published in 1997. The survey highlighted the fragmentation and diversity in most therapies. There are many small organisations representing graduates of particular schools.

The University has published a further report on the professional organisation of Complementary and Alternative medicine in the UK 2000, which is accompanied by an information pack, *Regulatory Prospects for Complementary and Alternative Medicine*. This publication aims to provide the representative bodies for CAM with a guide to regulatory processes in the healthcare community.

Some branches of complementary medicine are making great efforts to bring about co-operation amongst the different organisations in their profession. This is resulting in improved standards of training and greater public recognition. This applies particularly to acupuncture, aromatherapy, healing, herbal medicine and homoeopathy. Osteopathy and chiropractic are much further ahead. These two professions have achieved self-regulatory status which is officially recognised in two separate Acts of Parliament. As from May 2000, osteopaths are required to be registered with the General Osteopathic Council (GOsC) and pay an annual fee of £750. It is now illegal for practitioners to use the term 'osteopath' unless registered with the GOsC.

Umbrella bodies

The following umbrella bodies are working to further the interests of complementary medicine:

- The Institute of Complementary Medicine (ICM)

- British Register of Complementary Practitioners (administered by the ICM)

- British Complementary Medicine Association (BCMA)

- British Council of Complementary Medicine
- Council for Complementary and Alternative Medicine
- Association of Schools and Colleges in Complementary Medicine.

These organisations represent practitioners, professional associations and training establishments. They are working to raise the standards within complementary medicine and to further such issues as registration of practitioners and research.

University degrees in complementary medicines
Some universities are now offering degree courses in various therapies. Postgraduate degrees are also on offer, along with research opportunities. This will give complementary medicine the academic foundation it needs in order to become more integrated with the mainstream health-care system. See Chapter 4 and the Appendix for more information on university courses.

CASE STUDY

Putting therapies into the practice
'It is a huge success,' reported Dr McIvor. 'Jim sees five people per session, giving each one a half-hour treatment. People are experiencing improvements in their pain and mobility, and also other spin-offs such as better sleep, less anger and irritability, more energy. He's making a real difference'.

His colleagues nodded their approval. Employing a massage therapist was their first attempt to introduce complementary therapies into the practice. They had interviewed six candidates, all with different letters after their names. They had chosen Jim because of his enthusiasm, his previous experience as a physical education instructor and the fact that he had taken a thorough two-year full-time training course.

The doctors agreed to advertise for a reflexologist as their next step. Dr McIvor's wife had had great benefit from treatments and Dr Jones had found it excellent for his own stress symptoms. It would be suitable for those patients who preferred not to undress. 'Before we advertise, let's find out about the different qualifications in reflexology. We can then specify what we want in the advert,' suggested Mrs Impey, the practice manager. 'A sensible idea,' agreed Dr McIvor. 'That will save a lot of confusion.'

2

'Hands-on' Therapies

This chapter deals with those therapies which involve physical contact with clients. Scientific research shows that touch is beneficial to human health in many ways, even helping to strengthen the immune system. Attitudes to touching vary greatly. The traditional British reserve contrasts starkly with the openness of Mediterranean cultures, for example. In some countries, notably India and South America, baby massage is a normal part of family life. The benefits of baby massage are only just beginning to be appreciated in Britain.

The therapies described in this chapter involve varying degrees of touch. The acupuncturist needs a gentle touch to insert needles with minimum discomfort for the client. Most other physical therapists need both gentle and firm touch, along with technical skill and dexterity. Stamina is necessary too, particularly for busy osteopaths and chiropractors. Anyone considering a 'hands-on' therapy as a career needs to be fit and in excellent health.

ACUPUNCTURE

Acupuncture has been practised in China for some 3,500 years. Legend has it that acupuncture was discovered when it was noticed that soldiers who received arrow wounds in battle sometimes recovered from other long-standing ailments. Before the 1960s, acupuncture was virtually unknown in the UK. It really began to take off in the 1970s and 1980s and is now one of the most popular therapies.

Traditional Chinese Medicine (TCM for short) is based on concepts which are challenging for the Western mind. The acupuncture student will need to study **Yin and Yang** theory in great depth (see Figure 1). Yin is the female energy, associated with passivity, darkness, swelling, cold and dampness. Yang is the active male energy, associated with light, contraction, heat and dryness.

When Yin and Yang are out of balance within the body, illness can result.

The **Five Element** theory is another important concept. Fire, Earth, Metal, Water and Wood are each associated with the different organs, e.g. liver and gallbladder are linked with the wood element. Imbalances of the Five Elements result in disease. Diseases may be classified according to the **Eight Syndromes**: interior and exterior, hot and cold, deficiency and excess, yin and yang.

The acupuncturist must, of course, acquire a detailed knowledge of the **meridian system**. There are twelve main meridians and eight 'extra' meridians. Needles are inserted in selected points in order to rebalance the client's energy, or 'qi'. A wide variety of ailments may be successfully treated with acupuncture, e.g. back pain, arthritis, rheumatism and digestive problems. Acupuncture can also be used in the treatment of drug addiction and for giving up smoking.

Entry requirements: 5 GCSEs and 2 A-levels or equivalent. Applicants without these may have other qualifications and experience taken into account. Minimum age for entry is usually 21 years.

Length of course: 3 years intensive part-time for licentiate qualification. Tuition mainly at weekends. Some longer blocks of study are required, especially for the clinical practice in the third year.

The acupuncture syllabus typically includes:

- anatomy and physiology
- Traditional Chinese Medicine theory
- the meridian system, function and location of points
- diagnostic techniques, including pulse and tongue diagnosis
- types of needles and needling techniques
- hygiene and safety procedures
- other traditional techniques, e.g. moxibustion (burning a herb on selected points)
- electro-acupuncture (electrical stimulation of points)
- Chinese herbal medicine
- treatment of women, children, pregnant women, the elderly

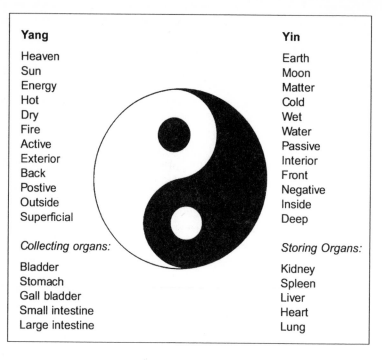

Yang	Yin
Heaven	Earth
Sun	Moon
Energy	Matter
Hot	Cold
Dry	Wet
Fire	Water
Active	Passive
Exterior	Interior
Back	Front
Postive	Negative
Outside	Inside
Superficial	Deep
Collecting organs:	*Storing Organs:*
Bladder	Kidney
Stomach	Spleen
Gall bladder	Liver
Small intestine	Heart
Large intestine	Lung

Fig. 1. Acupuncture theory includes the concept of Yin and Yang.

- acute and life-threatening conditions
- bereavement and care of the terminally ill patient
- patient management and treatment planning
- practice development and management.

Further professional development is strongly encouraged. The colleges offer a wide range of postgraduate courses in specialist areas, including acupuncture for animals.

AROMATHERAPY

Aromatherapy has enjoyed enormous growth over the last twenty years. It is, in fact, another ancient healing art. Aromatic substances have been used throughout history for treating common ailments and for religious rituals. It is widely acknowledged that the founder of modern aromatherapy is Rene Gattefosse, a Frenchman who burned his hand while working in a perfume laboratory. He plunged his hand into a vat of lavender and was amazed how quickly it healed. This led him to spend the rest of his career investigating the properties of essential oils.

Nowadays, aromatherapy usually refers to a massage treatment using a combination of essential oils specially chosen for the individual client's condition. The essential oils are diluted in a carrier oil, e.g. sweet almond or grapeseed, and are absorbed into the body through the skin. The client receives all the benefits of massage along with the benefits of the oils, which have a profound effect on the body and the mind. Aromatherapy is one of the best ways of combating stress and tension. A good treatment leaves one with a feeling of deep relaxation and well-being.

Many essential oils are powerfully antiseptic and are helpful for minor infections. The aromatherapist will advise clients on the use of essential oils in the bath, in compresses or inhalations. Oils, lotions and creams are sometimes made up for the client to use at home in between treatments.

Entry requirements: no formal educational qualifications are specified.

Length of course: varies from school to school. Full-time courses take 9 or 10 months, part-time courses 1–2 years.

The aromatherapy syllabus typically includes:

- anatomy and physiology
- full body massage, including basic lymphatic drainage; usually also includes acupressure points and foot reflex points
- essential oil production, aromatic plants, methods of extraction and quality assurance
- chemistry and toxicology of essential oils
- physical and psychological effects of essential oils
- study of 40–50 essential oils and a range of carrier oils
- blending of essential oils
- olfaction (study of sense of smell)

- consultation skills, case notes, treatment planning
- aromatherapy for common ailments
- practice management, business skills.

Aromatherapists are encouraged to attend postgraduate courses on specialised aspects of aromatherapy, e.g. aromatherapy for cancer patients, pregnancy, etc. Most aromatherapists set up in private practice working from home or a clinic. There are an increasing number of opportunities for sessional work within the health service.

Aromatology

This is a new specialism which involves the use of essential oils without massage. Widely used in France, essential oils are prescribed internally. This is now being taught in the UK to qualified herbalists, pharmacologists and medical staff. A strong scientific background is preferred for students of aromatology.

BOWEN TECHNIQUE

The Bowen Technique is a relatively new addition to the range of complementary therapies. It was developed in Geelong, Australia by Tom Bowen. Bowen had studied medicine and also worked as an industrial chemist. He became a full-time therapist in the 1950s, eventually treating over 13,000 patients a year, most of whom required only one or two treatments. In 1974 he invited Oswald Rentsch and his wife Elaine to study with him and document his techniques.

The Bowen Technique consists of sequences of moves applied to specific sites on muscles and tendons. The therapist uses fingers and thumbs to apply very gentle pressure. There is a short pause between each move. It is a subtle, relaxing and non-invasive technique, and can be performed through light clothing.

Sports injuries, repetitive strain injuries, frozen shoulder, back pain, migraine and asthma are some of the conditions which respond to treatment by the Bowen Technique. It is a method of stimulating the body's self-healing mechanism, relieving pain and tension and restoring balance. It is a completely safe technique which is suitable for people of all ages, including babies and the very elderly, and also for animals.

Entry requirements: no formal qualifications necessary.

Length of course: 9 months part-time. Before being allowed to practise, students need to obtain certificates in first aid and anatomy and physiology (these are not taught within the course).

The Bowen Technique syllabus:

- Tuition in the theory and practice of the various moves used in giving treatment.

The Bowen Technique is popular with practitioners who are already qualified in other therapies, e.g. osteopathy, but can be practised equally well by people with no prior training in complementary medicine. A technique for use with horses, Equine Muscle Release Therapy (EMRT), has just been introduced to the UK from Australia.

CHIROPRACTIC

Chiropractors specialise in correcting mechanical disorders of the spine and other joints. It is an ancient art. Hippocrates wrote about manipulation over 2,000 years ago.

Modern chiropractic was developed at the end of the nineteenth century in the USA by Daniel D. Palmer. He attributed the cause of much pain and disease to misalignment of the spinal vertebrae. This interrupted the flow of information from the nerves in the spinal column to the organs and cells. This could be corrected by manipulating the spine, thus restoring health. Palmer gave the first ever chiropractic treatment in 1895, which restored the hearing of the janitor in the building where Palmer worked. In 1896 he was jailed for practising without a medical licence.

Palmer went on to open a school of chiropractic, in the face of medical opposition. It was his friend, the Revd. Samuel H. Weed, who coined the term 'chiropractic', from the Greek words 'chieri' (hand) and 'praktikos' (performed). Chiropractic is now the third largest medical profession, after doctors and dentists.

Chiropractors work mainly on the spine, but can also manipulate other joints to correct any misalignment and restore mobility. Conditions which respond to chiropractic treatment include: all types of back pain, sciatica, headaches and migraine, sports injuries and repetitive strain injury, injuries to knees, ankles, shoulders, etc.

Pregnant women and children may also be treated. When necessary, the chiropractor will use X-rays to assist in diagnosis.

Like osteopathy, the chiropractic profession is now regulated by statute. The Chiropractors Act was passed by Parliament in 1994 and all practitioners must now be registered in order to practise legally in the UK.

Entry requirements: A-level standard required for school-leavers. Mature students assessed individually.

Length of course: 4–6 years. A shorter course (2 years 4 months) is offered at the University of Surrey for people who already hold a BSc in a biomedical science or are medically trained.

The chiropractic syllabus typically includes:

- anatomy and physiology
- neurology and applied neurology
- general pathology
- chiropractic diagnosis
- chiropractic techniques, palpation and biomechanics
- kinesiology (muscle-testing)
- X-ray physics, clinical imaging and normal radiographic anatomy
- psychology
- nutrition
- research methodology
- communication skills and the therapeutic relationship
- clinic management and business skills.

Chiropractic is a fast-growing profession. Incomes are higher than in most other branches of complementary medicine, and so are expenses. The sophisticated treatment tables, X-ray machines and other high-tech equipment used in the modern chiropractic clinic require a considerable financial investment.

Two colleges also run courses in chiropractic for animals for practitioners who wish to work in this field.

CRANIOSACRAL THERAPY

Craniosacral therapy has developed from the work of an American osteopath, Dr William Sutherland, who studied the moveable bones of the adult cranium, the spine, the sacral bones and the circulation of the cerebrospinal fluid. Dr Sutherland experimented on himself by finding ways of applying controlled pressure to various parts of his head. This produced head pains, problems with coordination and even personality changes. Dr Sutherland went on to develop a system of examination and treatment for the bones of the skull. This was the beginning of cranial osteopathy. However, the ideas were not taken up by the osteopaths, but were refined and developed by Dr John Upledger, Rollin Becker and others. Craniosacral therapy emerged as a separate discipline.

Trained therapists are able to detect with their hands the very slight rhythmical movement of the cerebrospinal fluid. They can identify any areas of congestion or restriction caused by stress, tension or trauma. Using a very light touch, it is possible to encourage the body to let go of firmly held patterns and to function more freely.

Craniosacral therapy is deeply relaxing and may be used to help a wide range of conditions, both physical and emotional. It is so gentle that it may be used for babies suffering from colic, sucking problems etc., which sometimes result from a difficult birth. It may also be used for painful conditions where other therapies may not be appropriate.

Entry requirements: courses are designed for practitioners of orthodox and complementary medicine who already have a good knowledge and experience of anatomy, physiology and pathology.

Length of course: generally 2 years part-time.

The craniosacral therapy course typically includes:

- the Primary Respiratory Impulse, the subtle inner pulsations identified by Dr Sutherland
- the detailed anatomy of the craniosacral system
- the detailed study of the nervous and endocrine systems
- study of fascia and fascial releases

- framework for diagnosis and treatment planning
- the effects of trauma on the craniosacral system
- contraindications to treatment.

Craniosacral therapy is an exceptionally gentle therapy which acts at a very deep level. It is now becoming much more widely practised and valued.

KINESIOLOGY

Kinesiology (pronounced kin-easy-ology) comes from the Greek word 'kinesis' which means 'motion'. The word relates to the study of muscles and the movement of the body, but in complementary medicine it now has a much broader meaning. An American chiropractor, George Goodheart, developed 'applied kinesiology' in the 1960s. He discovered that there were links between the muscles and acupuncture meridians. By applying gentle muscle tests, he was able to assess the condition of meridians, organs and glands in the body. He found that weak muscles could be strengthened by massaging reflex points, which then resulted in health improvements.

An associate of Goodheart's, John Thie, adapted this work to create 'Touch for Health'. This was a simple system which people without chiropractic training could use at home for family and friends. Touch for Health can be used to improve energy levels, ease aches and pains, release emotional stress and identify food allergies and nutritional deficiencies. An enormous range of different kinesiologies has grown out of this original work. Examples are:

- *Applied kinesiology* which is based on the techniques developed by Goodheart and other chiropractors in the USA. It is often used by osteopaths and dentists to treat physical complaints. AK has a wide range of applications, e.g. endocrine system imbalances, digestive disorders, allergies and immune system disorders, as well as structural problems of the neck and back. It can also be used for phobias and anxiety.

- *Educational kinesiology* to help children and adults overcome learning disabilities and dyslexia.

- *Health kinesiology* to alleviate problems caused by negative thinking, stress, allergies, geopathic stress, the electromagnetic effects of computers, televisions and other devices, problems caused by old physical injuries, etc.

- *Creative kinesiology*, which employs techniques to increase people's life potential.

Entry requirements: no formal qualifications specified.

Length of course: varies according to branch of kinesiology studied. Touch for Health may be learned in a few weekends, while a professional course in health kinesiology takes approximately 1 year part-time, and a diploma in applied kinesiology 2 years part-time.

The kinesiology syllabus typically includes:

- muscle-testing techniques
- corrections for strengthening weak muscles, e.g. neurovascular and neurolymphatic points
- acupuncture meridians and selected points
- meridian balancing techniques
- emotional stress release
- detecting and correcting allergies and nutritional deficiencies.

The different branches of kinesiology all have widely differing course content. Some courses include a range of techniques from different branches. Prospective students need to do some thorough research to ensure that the course will meet their needs. Because of its versatility, kinesiology is increasing in popularity. A good practitioner can help a wide range of physical and emotional conditions.

MASSAGE

Massage is the oldest of the healing arts. It was used in Greek and Roman times and the Chinese have used it for thousands of years. Hippocrates (460–370 BC) is reputed to have taught that 'Hard rubbing binds, much rubbing causes parts to waste and moderate rubbing makes them grow...' and 'Rubbing can bind a joint that is too loose and loosen a joint that is too rigid.'

There is, of course, much more to massage than rubbing. One gentleman who had had a great many massage treatments over the years was able to accurately guess how long each therapist had been in practice from the quality of the therapist's touch.

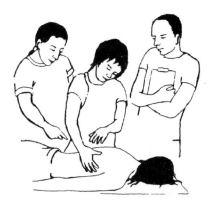

The Swedish professor, Per Henrik Ling, is generally regarded as the father of modern massage. He developed the techniques which he taught at his school in Stockholm. The term 'Swedish massage' refers to these techniques. Nowadays many terms are used, e.g. therapeutic, remedial and holistic massage. There are a great variety of massage styles and every therapist develops his or her own style through combining elements learned on different courses, from colleagues and from individual intuition.

The benefits of massage treatment include relaxation of body and mind, improved circulation of blood, lymphatic drainage, improved muscle tone and flexibility, and enhanced immune system. Besides promoting an overall feeling of well-being, massage can successfully target particular problems with joints and muscles and many minor ailments.

Entry requirements: no formal educational qualifications are required.

Length of course: varies from school to school. Generally 4 months to 1 year, depending on course. Tuition is mainly at weekends.

The massage syllabus typically includes:

- basic anatomy and physiology
- massage techniques: effleurage (long stroking movements), petrissage (wringing, kneading), friction (small, deep movements to soften nodules and to loosen joints), percussion (hacking, pounding techniques)
- developing a massage sequence

- use of oils, creams, lotions, etc.

- massage for common ailments

- clinical contra-indications (circumstances in which massage should not be given)

- client comfort and care, case histories and notes

- hygiene and safety

- the practitioner's posture and well-being

- building a practice.

There are many **specialised branches** of massage. Some therapists combine two or three, according to their own preferences and interests. The main specialities are:

- *On-site massage.* A shiatsu-style massage sequence which is performed with the client seated on a specially-designed portable chair. There is a growing demand for therapists to travel to office blocks, motorway service stations, large department stores, etc. Enlightened employers are realising that a 20–30 minute massage is very effective for reducing stress and tension and for improving concentration.

- *Sports massage.* Specialised training is available for people who wish to work in this area. Treatments are aimed at increasing suppleness and flexibility for sports enthusiasts in order to optimise performance. The sports masseur/masseuse will need to learn how to deal with the sprains, torn ligaments and broken limbs which occur on the sports field. The use of ultra-sound apparatus and other techniques is important here.

- *Baby massage.* Massaging babies and infants is an accepted part of the culture in many countries. It is recognised that there are benefits for both mother and baby. A gentle massage can help to calm a fractious baby and also helps to strengthen the immune system. Therapists often work in maternity hospitals and run courses to teach parents how to massage their babies.

- *Indian head massage.* This has become very popular in recent years. Traditionally used by women in India to keep their long hair in good condition, this type of massage employs particular oils and techniques to relax the head, face and neck. It takes only 20 minutes and can be performed with the client fully clothed and seated on an ordinary chair. The Indian head massage sequence can be learned in one or two weekends.

* *Manual lymphatic drainage.* The lymphatic system is the body's waste disposal system. Sluggish lymphatics can contribute to a variety of ailments. MLD is a specialised set of techniques developed by an Austrian named Vodder. A feather-light touch and gentle 'pumping' movements are used to encourage the flow of lymph. It is of great value in the treatment of cancer patients who suffer from oedema (swelling) of the limbs. There are courses available in the UK, but the advanced training is only available in Austria.

OSTEOPATHY

Osteopathy was founded in the USA in 1874 by Dr Andrew Taylor Still. Dr Still had trained in engineering and this gave rise to his interest in the mechanical functions of the body. He believed that disease occurred when the nerve and blood supply to the body's organs and tissues was interrupted, e.g. through muscle spasm or curvature of the spine. Dr Still's detailed knowledge of anatomy enabled him to develop effective manipulation techniques to realign joints and correspondingly affect other tissues.

A student of his, Dr Martin Littlejohn, pioneered osteopathy in Britain. He set up the British School of Osteopathy in 1917. There are now about 2,000 registered practitioners in the UK. The profession is regulated by the Osteopaths Act which was approved by Parliament in 1993. This gives osteopaths a similar status to doctors and dentists. The Act makes it illegal for unqualified practitioners to call themselves osteopaths, thus protecting the public, and all osteopaths must now register with the General Osteopathic Council.

The majority of patients go to osteopaths for treatment of back or neck pain. Conditions such as sciatica, arthritis, migraine and many others may be helped by osteopathy. It is also effective for sports injuries and other injuries to muscles and joints such as wrists, knees, shoulders or elbows. The osteopath will carry out an examination of the patient, assessing the range of movement in particular joints, before deciding which massage and manipulation techniques to employ.

Cranial osteopathy is used for some conditions, mainly those involving the head and face. Very gentle pressure is applied to the head, which helps to improve the flow of cerebro-spinal fluid. Cranial osteopathy is particularly suitable for babies and children, especially when the birth has been difficult.

Entry requirements: 2 or 3 good A-levels or equivalent, including science subjects. Mature applicants on individual merit.

Length of course: 4 years full-time, 5 years part-time, leading to BSc(Hons) degree.

The osteopathy syllabus typically includes:

- anatomy and physiology
- body mechanics
- neuroscience and neuro-musculoskeletal studies
- pathology
- clinical sciences
- psychology and sociology of health
- soft-tissue techniques and neuro-muscular techniques
- osteopathic adjustive techniques
- cranial osteopathy
- osteopathic diagnosis and evaluation
- case history taking and patient examination skills
- communication skills and the therapeutic relationship
- rehabilitative techniques
- clinic tutorials
- clinic management and business skills.

The newly qualified osteopath requires little capital to set up in practice. Equipment is simple and relatively inexpensive. However, annual registration fees must now also be taken into account. There is a growing demand for qualified osteopaths and opportunities are opening up within the health service. There are opportunities for further study (it is now possible to do an Msc in Osteopathic Care) and also for research.

REFLEXOLOGY

This is another ancient healing art. Drawings dated 2330 BC found in an Egyptian tomb show a reflexologist giving a treatment. The Native Americans and some of the primitive tribes of Africa were also aware of reflexology. The modern pioneers of reflexology were Dr William Fitzgerald and Mrs Eunice Ingham, who worked in the USA. A student of Mrs Ingham, Doreen Bayley, instructed many of the early practitioners in the UK and on the Continent.

Reflexology involves the massage of the feet in a very precise manner, working on the tiny reflex areas which relate to every part of the body (see Figure 2). These reflex areas are located on the tops, sides and soles of the feet. Reflexes corresponding to parts of the body which are out of balance are sometimes felt as 'crystals' underneath the skin on the sole of the foot. The patient will sometimes feel a sharp, painful sensation as particular reflexes are massaged. This will usually correspond to an organ or body system which is not working efficiently or is diseased. The reflexologist will treat the area in order to help restore balance.

Reflex points are also found on the hands. The feet are more sensitive and more responsive to treatment, but the hands are used if it is not possible to work on the feet.

Reflexology can be used to treat a wide variety of ailments, both chronic and acute. A skilled therapist can pinpoint problems with great accuracy. It is not necessary to be ill to have reflexology: it is very effective for health maintenance and preventative health care.

Entry requirements: no formal educational qualifications are necessary. Minimum age usually 18 years.

Length of course: varies from school to school. Generally 6 months to 1 year of weekend tuition.

The reflexology syllabus typically includes:

- history and origin of reflexology
- anatomy and physiology
- the reflex map of the feet and hands
- zones of the feet
- foot care

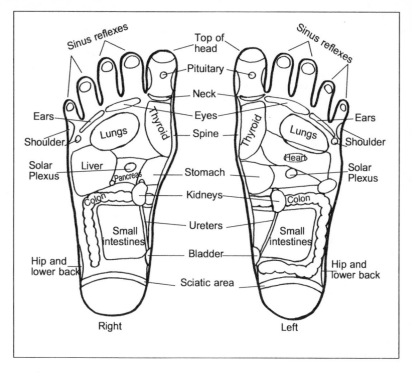

Fig. 2. Reflexology foot massage and chart.

- pressure techniques using fingers and thumbs
- treatment sequence
- client comfort and care
- reflexology for particular conditions
- consultation techniques, case note taking
- building a practice, business skills.

Research shows that reflexology is an effective therapy for many conditions. It is becoming more widely used in hospitals, clinics and institutions of all kinds. It is one of the most portable therapies. It requires no special equipment and the client needs to remove only shoes and socks or stockings.

REIKI

The word 'Reiki' means 'universal life energy'. It is a system of healing which has its origins in ancient Buddhist traditions and was reputedly used by priests in ancient Egypt and Tibet. It was rediscovered in the nineteenth century by a Japanese academic and Christian priest, Dr Mikao Usui. Usui had found a formula for healing and some symbols in Buddhist texts. He was shown how to use this information for healing on the final day of a three-week fasting and meditation retreat. Reiki was brought to the West in the 1930s by Hawayo Takata. It is very well-established in Europe and is enjoying a surge of popularity in Great Britain.

Reiki teachers are known as 'masters'. There are several slightly different systems of Reiki. The Usui system is regarded as the original one. Most people learn the first two 'degrees' of Reiki. One attraction of this form of healing is that it is very easy and quick to learn, though as with all therapies real skill comes with practice.

A Reiki treatment generally lasts for an hour. For most people it is an extremely relaxing experience which is said to be equivalent to 3–4 hours of deep sleep. The practitioner places his or her hands in certain positions on the client's head and then on the front and the back of the body. Most of these positions correspond to the endocrine glands. Each position is held for about five minutes. Distant healing techniques are also used.

As with spiritual healing, Reiki benefits all mental, emotional and physical conditions to some extent. In some cases it can produce remarkable improvements. It can help to strengthen the immune system and release long-held emotions. Most people experience a feeling of clarity, calm and well-being after a treatment.

Entry requirements: no formal qualifications needed.

Length of course: the first and second degrees are each taught in a weekend. Third degree and master training by arrangement with Reiki masters.

The Reiki syllabus typically includes:

- energy transmissions or 'attunements' given individually by the master to each student

- tuition and practice in the hand positions for treatments

- tuition in the use of the traditional symbols

- techniques for self-healing

- techniques for distant healing.

A portable treatment couch is required for giving Reiki sessions. The opportunities for Reiki practitioners are similar to those for spiritual healers and will undoubtedly increase as Reiki becomes more established in the UK.

SHIATSU

Shiatsu is a healing art which developed in Japan. It grew out of the ancient system of Oriental massage known as 'anma'. Shiatsu was traditionally used within the family and has only been used as a therapy for the last hundred years or so.

The word 'shiatsu' literally means 'finger pressure'. The shiatsu therapist applies pressure to the client's body with fingers, thumbs, palms, elbows and feet ('barefoot shiatsu'). Stretching techniques are also used to loosen the joints and stimulate the flow of 'ki' energy. The therapist works to bring more energy into the meridians or areas of the body which are depleted. Where energy has become

excessive or congested it is dispersed. By working with the energy flow in the body, the practitioner can help to restore balance.

Treatments are given on the floor using a futon. The client remains fully clothed and so is usually advised to wear loose-fitting cotton clothing, e.g. a tracksuit. Shiatsu treatments can be helpful for conditions such as back pain, headaches, digestive problems, stress and tension. Shiatsu helps to strengthen the immune system and so has a role to play in preventative health care. Giving advice on lifestyle and diet is an integral part of the shiatsu therapist's work.

Entry requirements: no formal educational qualifications stipulated. Courses are usually designed so that the introductory stages may be taken by people who do not wish to become practitioners, but are interested in self-development and wish to be able to help family and friends.

Length of course: 3 years part-time for practitioner qualification. Attendance requirements vary from school to school, but generally range between 80 and 100 days over the 3 years.

The shiatsu syllabus typically includes:

- anatomy and physiology
- oriental medicine theory: yin/yang, 'ki' energy, the meridian system, the Five Elements and much more
- oriental diagnostic methods including 'hara' (abdominal) and facial diagnosis
- practical shiatsu techniques to tonify, sedate or disperse ki
- 'ampuku', special techniques applied to the abdomen
- treatment of specific conditions, acute and chronic
- dietary principles (usually based on macrobiotics)
- case history taking, client/practitioner relationship, building a practice
- 'Do-In', a system of self-massage and exercise
- 'Qigong' and other exercises to develop the practitioner's own ki energy.

Shiatsu is becoming more popular and is gaining a good reputation. Most practitioners set up in private practice from home or complementary health centres. Career prospects look promising for the dedicated and enthusiastic practitioner.

SPIRITUAL HEALING

Throughout history it has been recognised that certain individuals have the ability to heal other people, animals and even plants. There are many references in the Bible to the 'laying on of hands'. Healing is a gift which many people have without even realising it. Some people have a quiet, soothing presence and find themselves often listening to the troubles of others, who go away feeling better. A lot of healing takes place in daily life and goes unrecognised.

Healing as practised by spiritual healers involves the channelling of healing energies to the patient. This may be done by laying on of hands or by absent healing. It works on all levels of the patient's being, i.e. physical, mental, emotional and spiritual. Some people feel nothing when receiving healing. Others feel tingling, a sensation of heat or sometimes coolness. Some people feel relaxed and others

Fig. 3. Diagram showing positions of the seven chakras.

re-energised. Healing has no side-effects, though some patients may feel worse for a short time as their stresses are released. It can sometimes bring about dramatic improvements. Healing can be used alongside other therapies, both complementary and orthodox.

Most physical and mental conditions can be helped in some way by healing. It can alleviate pain after accidents and surgery. It can also help with the effects of chemotherapy and radiation treatment. Healing certainly calms the mind. Sometimes healing can act as a catalyst, spurring the patient on to change outdated attitudes and patterns of behaviour. Even terminally ill patients can benefit. Healing can enable them to relax and find a sense of inner peace.

Entry requirements: no formal academic qualifications are necessary.

Length of course: varies according to teaching organisation. Usually consists of a series of weekend courses.

The healing syllabus typically includes:

- the aura (energy field surrounding the body)
- the seven chakras or energy centres (see Figure 3)

- spiritual attunement
- hands-on healing
- absent or distant healing
- meditation, visualisation and relaxation
- opening and closing the healing session
- personal development of the healer
- ethics and the healer's conduct.

A great many healers work for free or for donations. Those who choose to make a profession of healing charge similar rates to other practitioners. Healers are now found working alongside medical staff in a wide variety of settings including hospitals, hospices and doctors' surgeries.

ZERO BALANCING

Zero Balancing is a very modern therapy, devised by Dr Fritz Smith, an American who practised osteopathy and general medicine from 1957 to 1972. Dr Smith studied other disciplines during the 1960s and 1970s, including yoga, meditation and acupuncture. He devised Zero Balancing whilst studying acupuncture in England. It is a synthesis of the Eastern understanding of body energies and Western scientific knowledge of anatomy. The name 'Zero Balancing' came from a client who said after a treatment session, 'I feel I've been brought back to balance, like a return to zero.'

Zero Balancing can be helpful for a variety of skeletal and muscular problems. It is also effective for stress-related problems, facilitating the release of tension and emotional trauma held in the body. The practitioner carries out the treatment with the client sitting or lying, fully clothed, on a couch. Specific finger pressure and held stretches, called fulcrums, are applied to release and balance the energy flowing through the skeletal system. Treatment is focused on certain joints which have limited movement and are known as 'foundation joints', e.g. the sacroiliac and the tarsal joints in the feet. One of the unique qualities of Zero Balancing is that it enhances all other therapies and activities carried out with the hands.

Entry requirements: previous training in another therapy is strongly recommended for short courses. Prior qualification in another therapy or health care profession is required for the certification programme.

Length of course: two basic courses of 5 days each plus a 4-day advanced course. The certification programme requires written work and supervised practice, to be completed within 3 years.

The Zero Balancing syllabus includes:

- Zero Balancing theory
- Eastern energy concepts as related to bodywork
- the different types of touch: blending, streaming, channelling and interface
- Western anatomy from the energy perspective: the significance of joints and their energetic function
- contraindications for treatment; when to refer to medical professionals

There are still very few practitioners of Zero Balancing but numbers are set to grow steadily as the effectiveness of this therapy is more widely reported.

CHECKLIST

1. Are you comfortable touching and being touched?

2. How many 'hands-on' therapies have you experienced? In what ways did you benefit?

3. Which therapy appeals to you most? Can you say why?

4. Do you have the personal and financial resources to undertake a lengthy academic training for acupuncture, chiropractic or osteopathy?

3

Consultation and Teaching Therapies

This chapter deals with two groups of therapies:

1. therapies which involve a consultation with the client

2. therapies which involve teaching on a one-to-one or class basis.

Good communication skills are essential for practitioners of all the therapies in this chapter. Consultations in complementary medicine are often lengthy. A homoeopath, for example, may spend up to two hours with a client for the first appointment. It requires a great deal of concentration to be fully present with the client for the whole time. The practitioner must also have the ability to relate well to all kinds of people, some of whom will be in a distressed state.

Organisational skills are an asset for any practitioner. They are essential for anyone planning to teach in a class situation. Yoga and Tai Chi teachers need to learn how to handle groups and yet remain alert to the needs of individuals at the same time.

ALEXANDER TECHNIQUE

The Alexander Technique involves both hands-on work and teaching, and so overlaps Chapters 2 and 3. Strictly speaking, the Alexander Technique is not a therapy but rather a method of re-education. Teachers refer to their clients as pupils.

Frederick Matthias Alexander was an Australian actor who began to lose his voice on stage. Medical treatment was no help, so he watched himself in front of a mirror to see if he could find out what happened when he spoke. He noticed that he shrank in height, ducked his head and had problems breathing. This caused his throat to tighten. His body would react in this way even when he thought of speaking. Alexander found that by adjusting his thinking and his posture he was able to re-educate his body and regain his voice.

Alexander began to teach his technique to others and came to

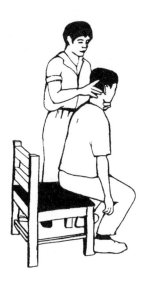

London in the early 1900s. At the age of 78 he had a stroke and managed to make a complete recovery using his own methods.

Teachers of the Alexander Technique usually begin by observing how their pupils stand, sit and move. They will then use their hands in a very gentle way to guide the pupil into better positions. The pupil gradually unlearns old habits and adopts easier, more relaxed ways of using the body. This unlocks tension held in the muscles and can help such conditions as back pain, tension headaches, high blood pressure, respiratory and digestive disorders.

Entry requirements: prospective students must have had a course of lessons with a recognised teacher prior to enrolment. No formal educational qualifications required.

Length of course: 3 years full-time, 4 years part-time.

The Alexander Technique syllabus typically includes:

- anatomy and physiology
- the study of F. M. Alexander's books and other literature
- body mechanics
- the relationship between Use, Poise and Posture
- the use of the voice
- practical hands-on training
- supervised teaching practice in third year.

The majority of Alexander teachers set up in private practice from their own homes or in centres and clinics. Some teach in the music and drama departments of universities and colleges.

AYURVEDIC MEDICINE

Ayurvedic medicine is the traditional Indian system of healthcare which is becoming increasingly popular in the West. The name comes from two Sanskrit words, 'ayur' meaning 'life' and 'veda' meaning 'knowledge'. It is a truly holistic system, embracing all aspects of physical, mental and emotional health. There is great emphasis on prevention and treating people before they actually become unwell.

Ayurveda identifies three basic constitutional types:

- **Kapha**, which has qualities of earth and water. People who are predominantly 'kapha' tend to be heavy with thick hair, and are generally cool, calm and complacent.

- **Pitta**, which corresponds to the elements of fire and water. Pitta types tend to be of medium build, with fine hair, and have a tendency to be forceful and express their anger.

- **Vata**, which has the qualities of air and ether. Vata types are often tall and lean, with dry hair and skin. They may tend to be 'spacey' and changeable.

Some people may be a combination of these elements, or 'doshas'. The Ayurvedic practitioner will determine which doshas are out of balance for the client, and will tailor the treatment accordingly. Treatments may consist of medicinal remedies made from herbs, minerals or foodstuffs. Massage, oil treatments, meditation, yoga and dietary regimes (including fasting) may also be used.

Entry requirements: varies according to level of course. Diploma course open only to qualified complementary therapists and health professionals.

Length of course: 3 year Diploma in Ayurvedic Medicine which includes a total of 6 months clinical experience abroad. Shorter courses available. Also 3 year degree (see Appendix).

The Ayurvedic syllabus includes:

- fundamental principles of Ayurveda

- anatomy and physiology

- principles of health and health promotion
- Ayurvedic herbology
- Ayurvedic methods of clinical examination
- therapeutic practices, e.g. yoga, meditation, nutritional counselling, marma-point therapy
- practice management skills, medico-legal and ethical issues.

Interest in Ayurvedic medicine is growing as increasing numbers of research studies show the efficacy of traditional Indian remedies and treatments. Demand for well-qualified practitioners is certain to grow.

BATES METHOD

The Bates Method of Vision Education is named after Dr William H. Bates, who was a respected opthalmologist in New York. He found that the vision of many of his patients was very variable. This meant that it could be improved. He gave up his orthodox practice to research and teach ways of improving eyesight without the use of spectacles. The Method has now been in use for over seventy years and has helped thousands of people all over the world to enjoy better eyesight.

Relaxation is the key to better vision. The Bates Method teaches clients how to relax the eyes and the mind whilst becoming more observant. Special techniques are used to give extra stimulus where needed and to integrate the use of both eyes.

Tired, sore eyes, long sight, short sight, astigmatism, squints and lazy eyes can all be helped by the Bates Method. Even such conditions as cataract, glaucoma, macular degeneration and retinitis pigmentosa may benefit from this approach. Teaching sufferers to use their eyes in the most normal and relaxed way can encourage healing.

Entry requirements: no formal qualifications needed. Prospective students should gain some experience of the Bates Method before enrolling on the Vision Education course. This may be through individual lessons, attending a workshop or the School's training clinic.

Length of course: 2 years part-time.

The Vision Education course includes:

- principles, history and philosophy of the Bates Method
- anatomy, physiology, optics
- the psychology of vision
- practical techniques including use of patches, lenses, grids and filters, stimulation through colour, contrast and light
- relaxation for the body, mind and eyes
- counselling skills and the use of flower remedies
- development of teaching skills.

Vision Education teachers usually set up in private practice. There is currently a great demand for teachers in all parts of the UK, but especially in the north and west of England.

COLOUR THERAPY

Colour therapy has been used in one form or another for thousands of years. The Luscher colour test has been used as a diagnostic tool by psychologists since the 1940s. The test consists of asking the patient to choose coloured cards. This reveals information about the patient's state of mind, e.g. orange and yellow indicate happiness and pink a tendency to self-criticism. The vibrational energies of colour are now finding their way into modern medicine, for example, the use of blue light to treat premature babies suffering from jaundice.

Colour is the visible part of the sun's electromagnetic rays. Each colour contains a variety of hues, each of which vibrates to a set frequency. Every person has his or her own electromagnetic field, or aura. Disease starts in the aura and manifests as an accumulation of stagnant energy, which is either devoid of colour or vibrating to the wrong colour frequency. If not eradicated at this stage, it will manifest as a physical illness. Reintroducing the correct colour frequencies may help to balance chakras and restore well-being. Some systems of colour healing associate certain colours with certain chakras.

The colour therapist may treat imbalances by irradiating the whole body, the spine or localised areas of the body with light of a specific colour, or by placing coloured fabrics on the body. The client may be taught how to perform visualisations with colour or how to breathe in colour. Advice may also be given about colour in dress, decor and diet. Some systems of colour therapy employ bottles of coloured fluid which clients may apply to correct imbalances.

Entry requirements: none specified.

Length of course: 1–2 years part-time.

The colour therapy syllabus typically includes:

- history of colour therapy
- physics of light
- anatomy and physiology
- the chakra system
- healing with colour
- counselling skills
- practice management.

Colour therapy combines well with many other therapies and seems set to grow rapidly in coming years as interest in all forms of 'vibrational medicine' increases.

CRYSTAL HEALING

Throughout history, crystals and gemstones have been prized for their beauty. Set in crowns and jewellery, they have always symbolised power and status. Many ancient cultures also credited crystals with healing powers, believing that they stored and conducted energies which resonated with the body and could facilitate healing. The unique energy-conducting properties of crystals are nowadays essential to the smooth functioning of our high-tech society. Microchips are made from silicon, rubies are used in laser technology and quartz crystals are used in clocks and watches.

When used for healing, quartz is considered to amplify and purify

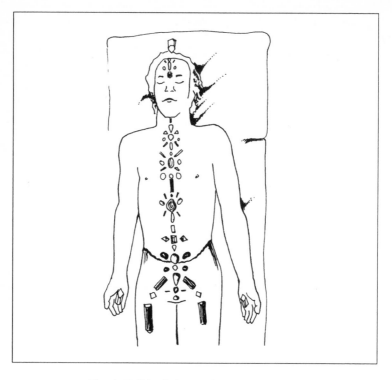

Fig. 4. Full body layout in crystal healing.

the subtle energies of the body. Certain crystals and gemstones are reputed to have affinities with the different chakras, or energy centres, e.g. turquoise resonates with the throat chakra and rose quartz with the heart chakra.

Crystal healing treatments are given on a couch or on the floor. There is no need for the client to undress. The therapist may hold crystals directed at the client, or may ask the client to hold them. Crystals may be placed on the body in positions corresponding to the chakras (see Figure 4). The therapist may also arrange crystals in a specific pattern or layout around the client in order to activate specific changes within the subtle anatomy. The skill of the therapist lies in choosing the correct crystals and configuration. The aim of the treatment is to energise and re-balance the body to create a state of harmony and well-being.

Entry requirements: no formal qualifications are required.

Length of course: 2 years part-time.

The crystal healing syllabus typically includes:

- anatomy and physiology
- scientific background of crystals and gemstones, crystalline structures, etc.
- the chakra system and subtle anatomy
- theory of vibrational medicine
- healing properties of crystals and gemstones
- practical use and care of crystals
- crystal patterns and layouts
- counselling and listening skills
- ethics and practice management.

Crystal healing is a branch of vibrational medicine. Some courses also include the use of flower essences and colour healing. Many therapists use crystals to amplify the effect of other healing techniques.

FLOWER AND GEM REMEDIES (VIBRATIONAL MEDICINE)

The use of remedies made from flowers has a long history. The Australian Aborigines used them over 10,000 years ago. The Ancient Egyptians and the Native Americans also used remedies made from flowers. Dr Edward Bach (pronounced 'batch') rediscovered the healing power of flowers in the 1920s. He was a respected Harley Street physician who also practised homoeopathy. Bach believed that emotions and states of mind profoundly affected physical health. His flower remedies, which he discovered through intuition, form a powerful system of psychological healing which may also help physical ailments in some cases.

Bach flower remedies are made by floating freshly picked flowers on spring water and leaving them in sunlight. The liquid is then drained off and bottled with brandy as a preservative. Scientific tests have shown that the remedies contain nothing but brandy and water. Bach believed that the healing vibrations of the flowers remained in the water.

There are 38 remedies, 12 corresponding to key personality types and 26 to different emotional states. The Bach practitioner makes up a mix of several remedies according to the client's current emotional state. Just four drops are taken, four times a day. The remedies work by bringing the subtle anatomy back into alignment.

In recent years many other ranges of remedies have been developed. British ranges include the Harebell, Bailey and Green Man Tree essences. There are also Californian, Alaskan and Australian Bush essences. Essences are also being made incorporating the vibrations of gemstones, light and the sea.

Bach Flower practitioner course

Entry requirements: open to all, but is aimed at people who are already practising therapists (e.g. aromatherapists, counsellors, reflexologists, etc.) or intending to become therapists. Applicants are expected to have a very good knowledge of the remedies before enrolling on the course.

Length of course: 4 days followed by 6 months of home study.

Bach Flower syllabus:

- in-depth study of practical application of the 38 remedies
- detailed case studies
- extended essay.

Vibrational medicine practitioner course

Entry requirements: no formal qualifications necessary.

Length of course: 1 year part-time for certificate, 2 years part-time for diploma.

Vibrational medicine syllabus includes:

- practical and direct experience of major families of flower and gem essences
- the subtle anatomy
- philosophy of vibrational medicine

- pathology and pharmacology
- basic first aid/mental health
- sensitivity and awareness training
- practice management.

This is a rapidly expanding field with new remedies being introduced all the time. Vibrational medicine may be practised on its own or in conjunction with other therapies.

HERBAL MEDICINE

All ancient civilisations had their traditional herbal remedies. The ancient Greeks, Romans and Egyptians were skilled in the art of herbal medicine. They took their knowledge with them as they travelled. Mediterranean herbs such as rosemary and lavender were brought to Britain by the Roman army. The North American Indians used herbs for healing and spiritual purposes. Herbs are still important in Chinese medicine and India has Ayurvedic medicine which uses herbs extensively.

In Great Britain many monks were skilled herbalists. Every monastery had its own 'physic garden' where herbs were grown. A great deal of herbal knowledge was recorded in the books of Nicholas Culpeper, who practised in the seventeenth century. In 1812 Henry Potter set up his shop in London to supply herbs and leeches. His firm is still supplying a range of popular remedies today.

The modern herbal practitioner may dispense herbs in their dried form for a 'decoction' or an 'infusion' which the client can easily

 prepare and drink. It is, however, more common to use tinctures, which are made by steeping herbs in an alcohol solution. The resulting medicine may not taste good, but there is no doubt that it does you good. Herbal medicine helps to stimulate the body's self-healing mechanism. It can bring about a more permanent recovery than drug therapy, though it sometimes takes longer to work.

Herbal medicine is effective for a wide range of conditions, e.g.

chest problems, digestive and urinary problems, arthritis and joint problems, infections and skin diseases of all kinds. Herbs also have a role to play in preventative health care.

Entry requirements: 2 or 3 A-levels, science subjects preferred. Other qualifications may be considered.

Length of course: 3 or 4 years full-time, 5 years part-time.

The herbal medicine course typically includes:

- anatomy and physiology
- clinical sciences
- biochemistry
- pathology
- philosophy of holism and healing
- botany, cultivation and identification of herbs
- herbal pharmacology, blending and prescribing of herbs
- preparation of tinctures, ointments, infusions, tablets etc.
- nutrition
- client care and case management
- communication and counselling skills
- herbal pharmacy and practice management.

Most herbalists set up in private practice. Some are now beginning to work within the health service. There are also opportunities for qualified herbalists to work in the research and development of new herbal medicines.

Note: Some of the acupuncture colleges offer training in Chinese herbal medicine. Many acupuncturists combine the two therapies.

Chamomile   St. John's Wort   Rose Hips

HOMOEOPATHY

The word 'homoeopathy' comes from two Greek words, 'omio', meaning 'same' and 'pathos', meaning 'suffering'. This relates to the principle which underpins homoeopathy, 'like cures like'. The founder of homoeopathy was a physician called Samuel Hahnemann, who was born in Dresden, East Germany, in 1755. He discovered that substances which produced certain symptoms in healthy people would cure those symptoms in sick people. Further research showed that the cures were quicker and more effective if the remedies were diluted so that virtually none of the original substance remained. Hahnemann listed the remedies in a book called the *Materia Medica.*

Homoeopathy was brought to Britain by Dr Frederick Quin, who had studied with Hahnemann. Dr Quin set up the first homoeopathic hospital in London in 1850. During the cholera epidemic of 1854 the hospital's death rate was 16 per cent, compared to 60 per cent in the general hospitals. Since then, homoeopathy has become one of the most respected complementary therapies and has been used by the Royal Family for many years.

The remedies used in homoeopathy are often derived from substances normally regarded as poisonous, e.g. arsenic and belladonna. They are usually given in the form of small lactose pills. The cure takes place from the top of the body downwards, from the inside outwards and from the most important organs to the least important. The symptoms which appear last will disappear first.

The skill of the homoeopath lies in accurately matching the client and the remedy. The first consultation will usually last for about one and a half hours. The practitioner needs to question the client closely to gather all the information necessary to prescribe the right remedy. Details such as moods, likes and dislikes for particular foods, feeling better in hot or cold weather, are all important information for the homoeopath.

Entry requirements: 2 A-levels for school-leavers. Other students must be able to show ability to follow a degree level course. Some colleges have a minimum age of 21.

Length of course: 3 or 4 years full-time, 4 or 5 part-time. Training is followed by a year under the supervision of an experienced homoeopath.

The homoeopathy syllabus typically includes:

- anatomy and physiology
- clinical medicine and effects of drug therapy
- history of homoeopathy
- the principles of homoeopathy, e.g. law of similars, the vital force, function and significance of symptoms
- the homoeopathic *Materia Medica*, symptom pictures of remedies
- homoeopathic case-taking and diagnostic skills
- treatment and management of cases
- counselling and communication skills
- research methods
- practice management.

There is a growing demand for qualified homoeopaths. It is still difficult to find a homoeopath in some parts of the country. Most practitioners set up in private practice but some are now working within the health service.

HYPNOTHERAPY

The word 'hypnosis' comes from the Greek word 'hypnos', meaning 'sleep'. The most well-known character in the history of hypnosis is the Austrian doctor, Franz Anton Mesmer (1734–1815), who treated people by putting them into a deep trance. Some of his bizarre methods brought him into disrepute but the word 'mesmerise' remains in the English language. In the early 1800s a few surgeons performed operations using hypnosis as the only anaesthetic. This technique failed to become popular due to the introduction of ether and chloroform.

In recent years there has been an upsurge of interest in the use of hypnotherapy as a cure for phobias of all kinds, for helping people to stop smoking, for eating disorders and for depression, panic attacks and anxiety. Scientific research has shown that hypnotherapy can help with pain relief in surgery, dentistry and childbirth. 'Gut-directed hypnotherapy' can be remarkably effective for irritable bowel syndrome. Hypnotherapy is also used for improving creativity, sporting performance, confidence, memory and concentration.

During a session of hypnosis, the therapist guides the client into a state of deep physical and mental relaxation. The client can choose to come out of this state at any time. At the end of the session, the client is gently returned to the normal waking state. Several sessions may be necessary to achieve the desired results. Many therapists combine hypnotherapy with various forms of psychotherapy. Some also make tapes for the client to use at home.

Entry requirements: degree or professional qualification in a caring profession preferred. Other applicants considered on merit.

Length of course: generally 18 months to 2 years part-time.

The hypnotherapy syllabus typically includes:

- the nature of hypnosis and altered states of consciousness
- preparing the client for hypnosis
- hypnotic induction and deepening techniques
- terminating the hypnotherapy session
- use of hypnosis for specific conditions, habit-breaking, etc.
- preparation and use of audio tapes
- psychological theory: study of the works of Freud, Jung, Adler and others
- ethical use of hypnotherapy and contra-indications
- practice management.

Hypnotherapists generally set up in private practice from home or in complementary health centres and clinics. Some are now working within the health service.

IRIDOLOGY

Iridology is a system of diagnosis using the markings on the iris of the eye. There is evidence to suggest that it was used by several ancient civilisations. As a young boy, the Hungarian doctor, Ignatz von Peczely (1826–1911) accidently broke the leg of an owl when he tried to capture it. He noticed a black line appearing in the owl's iris. This gradually changed to a black dot surrounded by white marks as the leg healed. Years later in his medical practice he noticed that patients suffering from the same illnesses had the same marks in the same place on their iris.

Dr Bernard Jensen, an American doctor, built upon the work of other researchers to work out a chart of the irises in the 1950s. This divides the iris into sections like a pie chart and also into six concentric rings. These sections correspond to the different parts of the body. The position of any abnormal markings shows which organ or body system is diseased or unbalanced. The texture of the iris also provides important information for the iridologist. An iris with fibres which are fine like woven silk shows a strong constitution. A coarse texture like hessian shows a weaker constitution.

The iridologist may use a torch and a magnifying glass to examine the eyes, or may take slides using a special camera. Iridology is a diagnostic method and is therefore used mainly by therapists who already have other skills, e.g. nutritional therapy or herbal medicine, which they can use to treat their clients. The client's progress can be charted through the iris. Iridology has a role to play in preventative health care, as potential weaknesses can be clearly seen in the iris.

Entry requirements: some schools will only admit students who are already qualified in another therapy and have studied anatomy and physiology.

Length of course: ranges from 3 months to 2 years part-time depending on the level of the qualification.

The iridology syllabus typically includes:

- history of iridology
- the anatomy of the eye
- diseases of the eye
- identifying constitutional types
- iris mapping
- reassessment technique.

Iridology is a useful and accurate diagnostic tool. It is a valuable skill for any therapist to acquire.

NATUROPATHY

Naturopathy, or 'natural cure,' is another ancient system of healing. Hippocrates' famous statement, 'Let food be your medicine and medicine be your food' is one of the guiding principles of naturopathy. According to the tradition of Hygieia, the Ancient Greek goddess of health, good health is normal when one lives in harmony with one's nature. Illness is created by the body rather than by external factors, and serves as a reminder to live a more harmonious life.

An early nineteenth-century pioneer of naturopathy was Vincent Priessnitz, who practised in Silesia in Eastern Europe. Priessnitz prescribed cleansing diets and enemas along with alternating hot and cold baths to stimulate the circulation. James Thomson and Stanley Lief brought naturopathy to Great Britain at the turn of the century. They both established residential clinics. Lief went on to open the British College of Naturopathy and Osteopathy in 1936.

Naturopathy works with symptoms, using them as a guide to treatment in order to restore health. A naturopath will not use medication to suppress symptoms. Practitioners believe that acute conditions are unavoidable and are the body's attempt to get rid of toxins. The methods used to restore the patient's health include diet, fasting, hydrotherapy, exercise, physical therapy, counselling, relaxation and rest. It is low-tech, low-cost treatment. The patient has joint responsibility with the practitioner.

Entry requirements: 3 A-levels including biology and chemistry or equivalent for BSc(Hons) Naturopathic Medicine. Mature students considered on individual merit.

Length of course: 4 years full-time for professional qualification.

The naturopathy syllabus includes:

• anatomy and physiology

- principles and philosophy of naturopathy
- soft tissue techniques: massage and physical therapy
- pathology
- diagnostic skills
- exercise physiology
- nutrition
- hydrotherapy: therapeutic baths, use of hot and cold water applications, Epsom salts, seaweed, etc.
- psychology and psychosomatic diseases
- immunology
- counselling skills
- clinical practice.

Naturopaths may set up in private practice or work in clinics or health farms. Many osteopaths also use naturopathy in their practice.

NUTRITIONAL THERAPY

Dietary deficiencies can cause serious diseases, e.g. a lack of vitamin C causes scurvy. Sailors on long voyages used to suffer from this condition until fresh limes and lemons were provided. This is an early example of nutritional therapy. Vitamin C has since been thoroughly researched, notably by the American biochemist Linus Pauling. He found that large doses of vitamin C could help cure the common cold and boost the immune system, bringing benefits for cancer patients.

Two other American researchers, Drs Hoffer and Osmond, used high doses of certain vitamins to treat schizophrenia patients in the 1950s. They achieved a success rate of 75 per cent. Research into nutritional therapy is now progressing at a rapid rate all over the world. Rarely a week goes by without some new study being mentioned in the media.

Nutritional therapy can help a wide variety of conditions, e.g. pre-menstrual syndrome, menopausal problems, food allergies, anaemia, and depression and other mental illnesses. Clients suffering from chronic conditions which do not respond to orthodox medical treatment, e.g. chronic fatigue, will often improve with nutritional therapy.

The therapist's task is to trace the client's medical history to discover how past lifestyle, illnesses and stresses have created his or her current state of health. The therapist can then devise a dietary programme with vitamin and other supplements to detoxify, strengthen and balance the client's system.

Entry requirements: none specified. Applicants considered on individual merit. A good understanding of science, particularly chemistry, is required for the longer courses.

Length of course: 1 to 3 years part-time.

The nutritional therapy syllabus typically includes:

- anatomy and physiology
- biochemistry
- philosophy of nutritional therapy
- pathology
- the chemical composition of foods
- vitamins, minerals and other supplements
- nutrition and allergies
- nutrition and the immune system
- designing diets
- designing supplement programmes
- communication and counselling skills
- practice management and business skills.

There is a growing demand for nutritional therapists. Most therapists set up in private practice from home or from a clinic. Some are now working for GPs and in the health service. There are opportunities in research and in the nutritional supplement industry.

TAI CHI

Tai Chi has enjoyed a great rise in popularity over the past few years. There are several different forms, the most well-known being the

'Hand Form'. This is the form which people practise in the parks early in the morning in China. Tai Chi is also a martial art and some forms use weapons such as swords and sticks. These styles of Tai Chi tend to be much more dynamic than the familiar Hand Form, which consists of slow, flowing movements.

Tai Chi and Qigong, which is somewhat similar, are both exercise systems designed to promote the smooth flow of energy (Chi or Qi) in the acupuncture meridians. When performed with relaxed breathing and a focused mind, the movements encourage muscular flexibility and suppleness, and benefit all the internal organs.

There are no teacher training courses for Tai Chi as yet. The Tai Chi Union of Great Britain is about to begin a pilot project to introduce certification. At present, anyone wishing to teach must first study with an experienced instructor for some years. New teachers must be seen to practise a recognised form of Tai Chi and to follow the true principles. They generally begin teaching their own classes on the recommendation of their instructor.

YOGA

Yoga is a Sanskrit word meaning 'yoke' or 'union'. It is an ancient system of exercises and spiritual practices which originated in India. The aim of yoga is to integrate the physical, mental and spiritual aspects of one's being. As long ago as 300 BC, the teacher Patanjali recorded the principles of yoga. His eight 'sutras' still form the basis of modern yoga teaching. For centuries, yoga was practised by a few people seeking spiritual enlightenment. Many modern students are indeed spiritual seekers, but the great majority practise yoga solely for the health benefits it brings.

There are several different forms of yoga. Raja yoga, for example, concentrates on mind control. Karma yoga is concerned with moral action. It is the system of postures or 'asanas' belonging to Hatha yoga which is most commonly taught in the West. The asanas are performed slowly and may be held for a short time to focus the awareness on the body. Regular practice brings flexibility, suppleness and relaxation. Breathing techniques (pranayama) and meditation also play an important part in Hatha yoga.

Yoga is an excellent method of preventative health care. It can also be used as a therapy. This aspect is now beginning to be recognised by the medical profession. Conditions such as asthma, back pain, arthritis and rheumatism, chronic fatigue, multiple sclerosis and other chronic ailments can be helped by yoga. It is also an excellent way to prepare the body for childbirth. Yoga teachers may choose to give general classes or to specialise in the more medical aspects of yoga therapy.

Entry requirements: no formal qualifications for general yoga teaching courses, but applicants should have attended classes with a recognised teacher for at least 2 years.

Length of course: 2 years to 2 years 6 months part-time for general yoga teaching.

> **Note**: A 2-year part-time course in yoga therapy is available for qualified yoga teachers. The emphasis of this course is on yoga for specific medical conditions.

The yoga syllabus typically includes:

- anatomy and physiology
- yoga philosophy and classical texts
- classical asanas
- pranayama breathing exercises
- kriyas: exercises to purify the internal organs
- the chakra system: the seven energy centres of the body

- meditations
- mantra: chanting sound vibrations
- teaching skills.

Yoga teachers organise classes in adult education centres, complementary health centres and many other venues. Some are employed within the health service on a sessional basis. Yoga therapists work with clients on a one-to-one basis. They may work with GPs, in hospitals and special needs centres as well as from home.

CHECKLIST

1. Are you a good listener? Can you hear what is not being said?

2. Do you communicate clearly and well with people from all walks of life? Can you put people at ease?

3. How many of the above therapies have you experienced? In what ways did you benefit?

4. Do you have the personal and financial resources to undertake a lengthy academic training for herbal medicine, homoeopathy, naturopathy?

4

Preparing to Become a Therapist

CHOOSING THE RIGHT THERAPY

With so many therapies to choose from, how do people make up their minds? The most common method is for the therapy to choose you. This happens in various ways. Every therapist has a different story to tell.

When the therapy chooses you

A teacher of the Alexander Technique
Ella had severe back problems for years. The doctors could only offer painkillers and an operation with no guarantee of success. In desperation, she went to the library to find out everything she could about the treatment of back pain. It was there that she came across a book on the Alexander Technique. She found a teacher locally and booked weekly lessons. Progress was slow but sure and within six months she was virtually pain free. The following year she decided to train as a teacher herself.

A massage therapist
Lindsay had a nervous breakdown following her husband's death in a road accident. After spending six weeks in hospital, she wanted to give herself a treat. A beauty salon in the town centre had a placard about aromatherapy in the window. Lindsay booked a treatment and experienced a wonderful feeling of calmness. Several more sessions followed. She became friendly with the therapist and spoke to her about training courses. Two years later Lindsay was working as a massage therapist alongside her new friend in a natural health centre in South London.

A homoeopath
Peter was frustrated at the repeated prescriptions for antibiotics for his son's ear infections. He looked at alternatives and came across

homoeopathy. The homoeopath prescribed remedies which worked on the infection and also seemed to bring other improvements in the boy's health. Soon the whole family was using homoeopathy, with good results. When Peter's mother died, he used his inheritance to finance a four-year training course. He now has a thriving clinic.

Reading about complementary medicine

Many people are introduced to therapies by reading magazines such as *Here's Health*, *Positive Health*, *Kindred Spirit*, *Caduceus* or the many other titles available at bookshops and newsagents. Anyone seriously interested in complementary medicine is advised to read one or more of these regularly. They are invaluable for learning about a wide range of therapies and keeping abreast of new developments.

Your local library is probably well-stocked with books on every aspect of complementary medicine. Do use this resource.

Making your choices

You may have a story to tell too. Perhaps your therapy has already found you. If not, take a large sheet of paper and jot down the answers to the following questions:

- Why do I want to become a therapist?

- Which therapies appeal?

- Why do those therapies appeal?

Make a **table of advantages and disadvantages** for each of the therapies you have listed.

And most important of all, make sure you **experience these therapies** for yourself. It is essential that you have a course of treatments from a qualified therapist. It is often a good idea to see two or three different practitioners over a period of time. This will enable you to get a real feeling for the therapy, and to assess the effects on yourself.

CASE STUDY

Jane chooses her new career

These are the notes Jane made when considering which therapy to choose:

'I want to be a therapist because I need to get away from the office environment and away from office politics. It's time for a change. This is an idea I have had for two years and it won't go away. My intuition is to act on it now.

Aromatherapy and shiatsu appeal.

I love essential oils and would like to learn more about them.

Shiatsu is a more vigorous therapy. I'm interested in the meridians, but could never be an acupuncturist.'

Jane listed the advantages and disadvantages of each therapy, as follows:

Aromatherapy: advantages
- qualify in 1–2 years

- course cost covered by savings in building society

- good course available locally.

Disadvantages
- lots of aromatherapists in area already

- only three or four really busy.

Shiatsu: advantages
- only one other shiatsu therapist in town, and she's doing well

- training involves fitness exercises

- lots of movement

- some meditation

- oriental approach.

Disadvantages
- 3-year course

- need to travel and stay overnight

- much more expensive.

Jane sent for prospectuses for both courses. She also booked in for an aromatherapy treatment and a shiatsu. She had experienced both in the past, but this time she really concentrated on what her intuition was telling her about each type of treatment. She also spoke to the therapists about their training schools and their experiences as students. In the end, she decided that it was shiatsu which filled her with the most enthusiasm and she could really imagine herself as a practitioner.

CHOOSING THE RIGHT COURSE

It is imperative that you choose the right course. If you get it wrong, you will jeopardise your future career and lose a lot of money in wasted fees. You will also lose valuable time. Time spent choosing the right course is wisely spent.

Sometimes people are drawn to particular courses through a set of 'coincidences'. You might see a course advertised in a magazine, then find that the person teaching it is giving a talk locally and is the best friend of someone you respect. When something like this happens, trust your instincts. The Universe often conspires to put us on the right path.

If you plan to study one of the major therapies, e.g. acupuncture, homoeopathy, aromatherapy, you will be faced with a choice of schools. How can you be sure of picking the right one? Here are some pointers:

Counting the cost

In complementary medicine as in everything else, you get what you pay for. A course which seems too cheap in comparison with others or which promises you a glittering new career after a one-week training is to be viewed with suspicion. If you are really serious about becoming a therapist, you must not allow yourself to be tempted by cheap, short courses. You run the risk of ending up with a diploma which is worthless.

Look at prospectuses from a number of schools. Find out what subjects are covered in each. Compare the fees charged and the length of each course. Go for the very best you can afford.

Trusting your first impressions

Your first communication with the school will tell you much. Whether you ring or write, your enquiry should be handled politely and promptly. Warning bells should ring if you leave an answerphone message which goes unanswered, or if the brochure you request takes a fortnight to arrive.

If the school is large and well-organised, offering three- or four-year courses in a major therapy, it will have its own premises and a full-time administrative staff. Courses in minor therapies which consist mainly of weekend seminars may be run from the teacher's own home, with tuition taking place in hired hotel rooms or halls. Details of the venues should be clearly set out in the school's literature.

The quality of the brochure or prospectus is important. If it is crisp, professionally printed and contains all the information a prospective student needs, then you can be reasonably confident that you are dealing with a reputable establishment. If the literature you receive is poorly written, full of typesetting errors, cheaply photocopied and barely legible, then enquire further before committing yourself.

Talking to the tutors

Good teachers exude enthusiasm and, in many cases, a fair bit of charisma. It is important that you meet the people who will be teaching you. Most of the large colleges hold open days for prospective students. A personal visit will give you the opportunity to judge whether you will get on well with the teachers personally, and to find out whether they inspire confidence and trust. You will be able to enquire about their background, how long they have been in practice, where they trained, and what special interests they have. This information may well be contained in the college prospectus.

You will need to know about the **philosophy** of the school and its teachers. Many therapies are based on ancient traditions and there are particular strands within these traditions, e.g. Iyengar yoga and Hatha yoga, acupuncture based on the Five Element theory and acupuncture based on Yin/Yang and Eight Principle theory. These separate branches of knowledge are often very different in approach and outlook. Some are very strict and traditional, whilst others have been adapted to suit the Western way of life. Seek out the course and the teachers whose ideals most appeal to you.

Nowadays there is an increasing emphasis on professionalism in teaching and most people setting up schools will have gone to the trouble of getting a teaching qualification such as a Cert. Ed. or the City and Guilds certificate in Further Education Teaching. It does not necessarily follow that a superb therapist who has a lovely personality will also be a good teacher, though this is indeed the case with some gifted people. Ask about **teaching qualifications** and try to make some assessment of the technical competence of the teachers you meet.

Contacting past graduates

Ask to be put in touch with a few past graduates of the school. They will be able to fill you in on the quality of the teachers, their strengths and weaknesses. Ask too about the quality and quantity of handouts and learning materials and whether the school is sufficiently well-equipped with treatment tables, audio-visual equipment, etc. Ask how much individual attention is given to students. Don't forget that past graduates are a mine of information about the best places to stay, where to eat, and other practical matters.

The most important question you will want to ask past graduates is naturally, 'How well did the course prepare you for setting up your own practice?' Ask questions about the content of the course. Was everything covered in sufficient depth? Was there enough emphasis on practical skills? How well were students' grievances handled? You will also want to know whether there is any provision for continuing supervision and support for new practitioners. By now you should have a pretty good 'feel' for the school and its staff.

It is important that you also get some idea of how well the school is managed. Ask past graduates whether there have ever been any financial irregularities, as far as they are aware. It would be disastrous if the school went bankrupt before your training was complete.

Understanding the qualification

Be absolutely sure that you understand the qualification that the school offers. Which letters will you be able to put after your name? Are these widely recognised within the profession? If the qualification is not the best in the field, will you be happy with it? Is it a degree-level qualification validated by a university? Is it a nationally recognised diploma? And if there is any possibility that you might work abroad, will your diploma be valid?

> **Note**: See Appendix for details of current degree courses in complementary medicine.

MAKING YOUR APPLICATION

Now that you have found out as much as you can about the course, you need to submit your application. Check that you have the necessary **entry requirements** first. For training courses with a very academic content, applicants may be required to have 5 GCSEs and

2 A-levels or the equivalent. Applications for undergraduate courses at universities must be made through the Universities and Colleges Admissions Service (UCAS).

There is generally a minimum **age restriction** for students on complementary medicine courses run by private schools and colleges. Many schools specify a minimum age of 21. One reflexology tutor prefers her students to be over 25 as she considers life experience to be an important factor.

Some schools are willing to accept students **without formal qualifications** if their previous experience and personal qualities are suitable.

> **Note**: A **scientific background** is necessary for some courses, e.g. nutrition. If you do not have this, you may be asked to take a science foundation course to bring you up to the required standard.

Whilst **application forms** for some minor therapies are usually quite straightforward, those for the major therapies can be quite searching. One acupuncture college asks questions such as:

- Please say why you have chosen to apply to this college.
- Why do you wish to study acupuncture?
- Do you have any experience of this or other therapies?
- Please give a brief description of your overall health.
- What are your present personal/work commitments?

Take enormous care with your application. Think about your answers and draft them out in rough before transferring them to the form. Remember that there is stiff competition for places at some colleges.

Attending the interview

A personal interview will usually take place before you are accepted. This will enable the teachers to question you in some detail about your motivation for doing the course, your commitment, your suitability as a practitioner and your ability to cope with an intensive course of study.

Prepare yourself for the interview as well as you can by reading the school's brochure and reading about the therapy. Have a few questions ready to ask the interviewers. Apply the same rules as you would for job interviews – arrive in good time, dress appropriately and comfortably, make good eye contact, smile. Let your enthusiasm shine through.

If you know you will be nervous, take a few drops of Rescue Remedy. Tissue salt No. 6, Kali Phos, which is available from health food shops, is good for butterflies and nervous headaches.

FINANCING YOUR STUDIES

You will need to raise a substantial amount of money if you intend to study one of the major therapies. This is an investment which you will recoup many times during your career.

Budgeting for additional expenses

Add on the cost of travelling, accommodation and meals. You may be able to share a car with other students, someone on the course may be able to put you up, think about taking as many packed meals as you can to cut down the expense. Bear in mind that books are likely to be a major expense. You may need some very specialised texts which may cost £20–£50 each, as well as charts and other equipment. Books can sometimes be bought second-hand, so keep your eye on the college noticeboards.

Career Development Loans

These are a possible source of finance for complementary therapy courses. The loans are available through a partnership between the Department for Education and Employment (DfEE) and four high street banks: Barclays, The Co-operative Bank, The Royal Bank of Scotland and the Clydesdale. They generally cover up to 80 per cent of fees plus books, materials etc. for courses of up to 3 years duration. The minimum loan is £300, the maximum is £8,000. While you are studying, and for at least a month after the course has finished, the Government pays the interest on your loan. If you find yourself unemployed at the end of the course, they will pay the interest for up to 18 months. When you do start paying it back, it will be at a competitive commercial rate of interest and will be spread over 1–5 years.

Information may be obtained from the above banks and from Jobcentres, or ring Freephone 0800 585 505. The banks and the DfEE have strict criteria for awarding Career Development Loans. If you are turned down by one bank, try another. It is possible that some courses may not be considered suitable, so apply several months before the course begins in case you have to make other arrangements.

Local Education Authority Awards

Full-time UK undergraduates may be eligible for an award from their LEA towards the cost of course fees. This will normally be dependent upon your own, and if appropriate, your parents' or spouse's income. Apply to your LEA as soon as your place on the course is confirmed.

Student loans

Full-time UK undergraduate students are eligible to apply for student loans. In order to obtain a loan, you must apply to your Local Education Authority (LEA). The amount you are allowed to borrow will depend, to some extent, on your family income. Student loans are an efficient form of debt finance, since the interest rates are linked to the retail price index and are lower than commercial rates. After your course, you will not be expected to make repayments until your income reaches a certain level.

Other methods of financing your course

- The Individual Learning Account Scheme was introduced by the Government in June 2000 and may provide help with some types of course. It is financed by the Government and administered by local Training and Enterprise (Skills) Councils, and offers a one-off payment in vouchers towards continuing vocational training. You must be 19 or over to apply, and not enrolled on a full-time course. You will need to pay the first £25 of the training yourself. The provider of the training must be registered with the scheme. Ring Freephone 0800 072 1072 for more information.

- The rate of interest on **credit cards** is generally higher than for other forms of borrowing. Some schools will accept credit cards as a method of payment, so this may be another way of spreading the cost of some courses over a period of time.

- Finding **sponsorship** from a company or amongst your personal contacts is another possibility. It would be vital to be sure that the finance would last until the end of your training.

- Small sums are often available from local **trusts** and **charities**. Larger trusts and charities may be prepared to help, but you may need to show that you have begun the course and obtain references from the school first. Your local library will have lists of trusts and charities, and the school might also have contacts.

Have you got enough money to finish?

For your own peace of mind, you need to be sure that you have adequate finance to complete your course. There is nothing more heartbreaking than running out of funds halfway through. Most schools will do their best to help students who run into financial difficulties. Some have student bursary funds to help with this sort of situation.

Making sacrifices

If you intend to study whilst continuing with your full-time job, be aware of the sacrifices you will have to make for the duration of the course. You may not be able to afford your normal holidays, but then you will need to use some of your holiday time to stay at home and study. Accept that your social life will be severely curtailed, but it will be cheaper to stay in and study than to go out to the pub or cinema.

CASE STUDY

Owen considers his options

'I've always been very academic and my parents wanted me to follow the family tradition by going into medicine. My father is a doctor and my uncle is a surgeon. I went along with their wishes but knew I'd made the wrong decision after two years at medical school. The complementary therapies attracted me more, especially after having acupuncture and osteopathy for a rugby injury.

'I sent away for prospectuses for the main therapies and was pretty impressed with what I received. The colleges seem to be well established and well run. I attended open days at some of them. Going along to the colleges really helped me to make the right decision. I got on brilliantly with the staff of the osteopathy college and knew immediately that I would get on well there. I was impressed with the premises and they were very well equipped. There was a good atmosphere in the place.

'Talking to the students enabled me to find out what the course involved. They were really positive about it. They were obviously working hard and having fun at the same time. My two years of medical training will actually be useful too. Everyone emphasised that career prospects are good, and the qualification is degree level. I've decided to go for it. Let's hope they'll accept me.'

CHECKLIST

1. **The therapy**: is it definitely the right one for you? Have you researched thoroughly? Had some treatments, done the reading, talked to qualified therapists?

2. **The school and the course**: are you satisfied with the reputation of the school and the credentials of the teachers? Is the course well organised, giving a thorough grounding in practical and theoretical aspects of the therapy? Do you wish to pursue a full university degree course?

3. **Past graduates**: are you pleased with the comments of past graduates of the school? Do they have successful practices?

4. **The qualification**: is the diploma well known and respected? Will you gain membership of a good professional organisation?

5. **Finances**: have you sorted out how you will pay for your course? Have you budgeted for extra expenses? Are your plans water-tight?

5

Training to Be a Therapist

ORGANISING YOUR STUDIES

Once you have secured a place on the course of your choice, you will naturally be filled with excitement. You will be able to look forward to fulfilling your ambitions and having some fun along the way. The new friends you meet are likely to be true kindred spirits. When the euphoria wears off a little, you may begin to wonder what you have let yourself in for. The sheer volume of information to be learned may cause a slight panic. Relax. You know you can do it, and you know you are going to enjoy it.

Colleges teaching those therapies with a great deal of academic content are aware that many students will not have done any serious studying for years. They therefore provide tuition on **study methods** and the best ways of organising course work.

Here are a few hints for studying. If you need more, refer to one of the many books on study techniques.

Managing your time

Before enrolling for the course, you will have been given some indication of the amount of time students are expected to spend studying each week. Students of acupuncture are advised to spend around 20 hours a week on home study, in addition to attending classes. This is a demanding four hours a day, five days a week. If you have a full-time job, you will need to plan carefully in order to fit this in, and there will be weeks when you will find it impossible to meet your quota of study hours.

Try to develop good study habits right from the start. Sitting down to study at regular times will help you to get into a good routine. The evenings are likely to be the main study time for most people, but you might find that you work well early in the morning. Perhaps you could use your lunch hour for reading or completing shorter tasks?

Making a study programme

Once the course has begun and you have been given an outline of your term's work, make yourself a plan of how much time you have available and decide, on a weekly or fortnightly basis, which task you will do when. This will help you to work steadily and consistently and to have assignments ready on time. Allocate certain times for reading, other times for written work, and make space for learning.

Help with remembering

Use your imagination to help with memorising facts. One osteopathy student pinned diagrams of muscles on the kitchen wall (see Figure 5). An aromatherapy student pinned lists of the chemical constituents of essential oils on the bathroom door. Doing this sort of thing might stretch the family's tolerance, but if it imprints the necessary information on your memory, it will be worth it.

Creating the right environment

You will study more effectively if you have a room or part of a room which is reserved for your work. There is nothing more frustrating than having to clear away your books halfway through a task because you are working on the family dining table. An area which is yours and which everyone else respects is much more conducive to serious study.

Organising your papers

Create files for every aspect of your studies so that papers can be kept well organised. Have the files and your textbooks on shelves or in a bookcase in your study area so that everything is to hand. Take care not to let clutter accumulate in your study area as this will frustrate you and distract you from your work.

Getting nowhere?

All students have times when nothing will sink in and everything they write seems to come out the wrong way round. When you hit times like this, take a break. Go for a brisk walk, do some exercise or gardening. Practical tasks will get you grounded again. If this does not do the trick, try to discover what your block is.

- Do you lack confidence in your abilities? If so, try taking some Larch, one of the Bach Flower Remedies for lack of confidence.

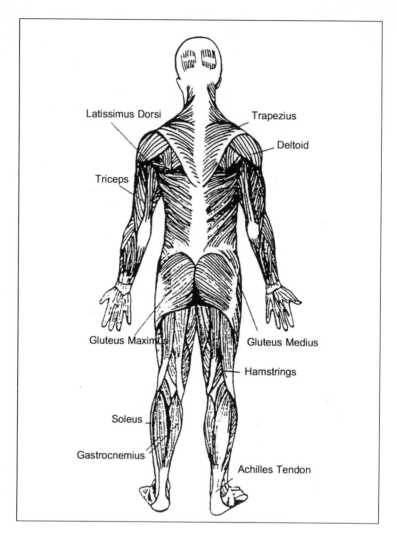

Fig. 5. Diagram of the muscular system.

- If you are feeling overwhelmed, Elm might be more appropriate.

- For workaholics who suddenly seize up, Oak may be helpful.

- Scleranthus calms and focuses a grasshopper mind.

Essential oils can also be useful if you find you are unable to concentrate. Rosemary is the best oil for stimulating the brain cells, followed by peppermint and basil. Try putting a few drops in a burner to fragrance the room, or simply put a couple of drops on a tissue and inhale. Best not to use these late at night, unless you want to burn the midnight oil, otherwise you might have difficulty sleeping. When you want to unwind after a session of serious studying, use lavender or sandalwood.

> **Note**: If you use a pottery burner with a nightlight candle, don't leave it unattended or put it too close to papers. One student of Traditional Chinese Medicine looked up from her text on 'Liver Fire Rising' to find flames coming from her oil burner, about to ignite her term's work.

Asking for help

If at any time you feel that you simply cannot cope with some aspect of the course, do not hesitate to contact your tutor and ask for help. Your tutors are there to guide you and will generally do their utmost to help students with advice or extra tuition. It is in their interests to help students make a success of the course. A ten-minute chat could save you hours of anguish.

PUTTING THEORY INTO PRACTICE

There will come a time when you will be asked to try out your skills on the public. You will not be asked to do this until your tutors know you are ready. They will carefully prepare you by getting you to work on fellow students in class first. You will be taught the essentials of the **therapist/client relationship**, how to take **case histories** and how to keep **client records**. The submission of case studies forms an integral part of every complementary medicine course and counts towards the diploma.

Students of herbal medicine, homoeopathy, osteopathy, chiropractic and acupuncture will have their practical work carefully controlled and monitored by their tutors. Their first contact with clients is likely to be in the college's teaching clinic under the watchful eye of a tutor. For some therapies this will not begin until the last year of the course.

There are schools which have well-established clinical **placement schemes** for students. These offer excellent opportunities for gaining good experience with clients suffering from particular conditions. One school of massage sends students to the cardiac ward of a local hospital. A school of shiatsu has contacts with substance detoxification centres, hospitals and clinics.

Finding guinea pigs

Students of healing, massage, aromatherapy and other bodywork therapies will find themselves needing to practise on guinea pigs between classes at a fairly early stage in the course. Your immediate family may or may not be ready to help. Friends and acquaintances are probably a better bet. If you belong to a group of some kind, perhaps a yoga class or a gym, put the word around that you are looking for volunteers. Make a point of working on a variety of people. You will need experience with young and old, slim and obese, male and female.

> **Note**: Remember that you must not charge for your services until you are qualified and properly covered by professional indemnity insurance.

The sessions with your guinea pigs are an important part of your training, helping you to gain experience and confidence. Treat them as an opportunity to put yourself into therapist mode. Wear your white coat or overall if appropriate. The whole procedure should give you a feeling for the way your working life will develop and confirm that you are on the right path.

Learning to take case histories

You will need to take a thorough case history even if you are working on a friend you have known for years. You will be guided on the correct procedure by your tutors. The case history will include:

- details of past ailments, including childhood illnesses, accidents, etc.

- family medical history if appropriate

- any hospital admissions/operations

- any current medication

- present state of physical health/symptoms

- present state of emotional/mental health

- information about the client's lifestyle, e.g. occupation, diet, exercise, etc.

Different therapies require different approaches to taking case histories. The case history for a massage treatment may take just 10–15 minutes. Up to two hours may be required for a really thorough homoeopathic case history. Collecting the right information from the client is an important skill. It enables the practitioner to make an accurate diagnosis and give the most appropriate treatment.

Presenting case studies

Your tutors will ask you to present your case studies in a given format for assessment. These will form an important element of your course work. The number of case studies required will vary according to the therapy you are studying. Massage and aromatherapy courses may ask for ten or twenty, other courses may require many more. Some may consist of single treatments. Others may need to be spread over a course of treatments in order to chart the client's progress. This will be specified by your tutors.

You will need to keep careful records of the **oils, herbs, remedies and/or techniques used**, and your reasons for using them. Your tutors will be looking for proof that you have understood the course material and are able to put it into practice effectively and efficiently.

They are also concerned with your ability to **relate well** to your clients. It is vital that you are able to inspire confidence in your clients and put them at ease. You must be able to listen to them attentively and empathise with them. It is also important to record feedback from your clients and carefully note any comments about the results of the treatment.

Your case study work will lay the foundations for successful practice later on. Most students find this the most enjoyable part of their course. It is where you really get to grips with the therapy you are studying. It also provides valuable training in planning treatments and working to strict appointment times.

Finding a mentor

By far the best way of getting professional feedback and advice is to enlist the help of a friendly local therapist who has time to spend with you. He or she will know exactly what to look for when receiving treatments and will be able to offer constructive criticism. It can be invaluable to have an arrangement like this with someone who can act as a mentor during your training.

TAKING YOUR FINAL EXAMS

Eventually you will reach the climax of the course, the qualifying examination. Here are two possible scenarios:

1. Being an experienced and well-organised student, you will have your revision plan prepared months in advance and will work steadily and methodically as the exam approaches. You will remain calm and unruffled, confident of success.

2. You will leave everything till the last minute and spend the night before the exam burning rosemary, drinking coffee and swotting furiously. You will be an emotional wreck, convinced of failure.

These are, of course, two extremes. Most people will manage something in the middle, i.e. generally well-organised but with moments of sheer panic.

Planning your strategy

Think back to exams you have taken in the past and remember what you handled well and what went badly. Apply your past experience to your present situation. Add to this everything your course has taught you about handling stress and you should be able to come up with a reasonable plan of action. For one person this might be three hours study every evening, followed by a relaxing bath and a fairly early night. For another it might be a vigorous game of squash followed by studying till the early hours of the morning.

Exam technique

On the day of the exam, do make sure that you **read the questions properly**. So many students come to grief by answering different questions from the ones on the paper. If you are apprehensive and nervous in spite of all your preparations, it is very easy to misread **instructions**. Work out how much **time** you have to answer each question and plan accordingly.

    Practical exams require similar attention to detail. You will need to show the examiner that you have the ability to prepare treatment couches or other equipment efficiently and also keep the work space well organised. Again you will need to work to a tight time schedule. The examiner will also be looking at your ability to relate well to your client, whom you will probably not have met before. By focusing all your attention onto the client and the task in hand, you will forget your own butterflies.

FRAMING YOUR DIPLOMA

Receiving your diploma is an exciting event. The larger colleges hold graduation ceremonies to which you can invite family and friends. This is the culmination of all your hard work. Put your diploma in a frame and hang it in your treatment room with pride. Now you are a fully fledged practitioner, a qualified professional. This brings with it some definite responsibilities.

JOINING A PROFESSIONAL ASSOCIATION

The first thing you must do is to arrange insurance cover so that you can practise. Your diploma will entitle you to become a member of the professional association for graduates of the school you attended. Some of the larger schools have their own associations. Smaller schools will usually have connections with a particular body which has approved their courses, e.g. some schools of aromatherapy are affiliated to the International Federation of Aromatherapists (IFA), others to the International Society of Professional Aromatherapists (ISPA) or to the Register of Qualified Aromatherapists (RQA). All such bodies aim to represent the interests of practitioners and to protect the public against malpractice by regulating standards and ethics.

Your membership will give you, for an annual tax-deductible fee:

- Professional indemnity insurance. This will provide cover in the highly unlikely event of being sued by a client. If you sell any products as part of your business, you should also be able to obtain public liability cover for this.

  Note: There are a few specialist companies offering insurance for complementary therapists. If you prefer to obtain insurance in this way, you should be able to pay a reduced membership fee to the association.

- The right to put letters after your name.

- A regular magazine to keep you abreast of developments in the association and within the profession as a whole.

- Access to annual general meetings and conferences.

- Access to postgraduate courses and seminars.

- A certificate of membership which may be framed and hung in your treatment room alongside your diploma.

If you wish to become involved in the organisation of your profession, you could eventually consider **standing for election** to the committee of the professional body. There are often several committees in the larger ones, focusing on issues such as education, research, etc. Such involvement is a good way of getting your voice heard and it also benefits your CV.

Professional associations also operate a system of practitioner **referrals** and **recommendations**. They are often the first point of contact for members of the public, clinics, health clubs, hospitals, etc. who are looking for a practitioner in their area. It is therefore vital that you ensure your professional association has up-to-date details about your practice at all times, and to inform them of any special areas of interest or experience you may have.

Abiding by the code of ethics

As a member of a professional association, you will be obliged to abide by a code of ethics. This is for your own protection and also serves to protect the public against any kind of malpractice. Be sure to obtain a copy from your school before you commit yourself to the course. Some codes set out in great detail exactly what is expected in terms of professional behaviour and standards. Whilst this provides a clear legal framework for therapists, it can sometimes seem restrictive, e.g. some codes have clauses preventing graduates from teaching for other schools.

Breaking any of the terms of the code may result in your dismissal from the professional association, leaving you unable to obtain the indemnity insurance you need to practise. Grounds for dismissal include professional misconduct, committing an indictable offence, or failing to renew your insurance cover.

CASE STUDY

Alan makes the grade

'There were times when I really didn't think I was going to make it,' admitted Alan. 'It was years since I had done any serious studying and concentration was a problem to start with. It was impossible to do any work until the children had gone to bed. The low point came halfway through the second year. The initial excitement of the course had worn off and the end seemed ages away. There were so many assignments and essays, I felt quite pressured at times. I almost gave up, but my wife Jan encouraged me through the bad patch. Thank goodness she did. When we came to do case studies, I really began to enjoy the course again.

'One excellent aspect of the course was the friendship and support of the other students. We shared so many experiences together. We're all planning to meet up at the annual conference soon. The tutors were always a great help too.

'Money was a worry, and still is because I'm paying back the loan Jan's father gave me. I'm doing some part-time work until the practice expands. The way things are going, I'll be a full-time herbalist by the end of next year. Clients are starting to come by recommendation now. Seeing clients improve over the weeks is so satisfying. It's good to be able to put all my training into practice at long last.

'I would encourage anybody to go into complementary medicine, but would advise them to build up some savings first. When you become interested in holistic health, your view of life changes. I am more relaxed now than I ever used to be. How did I stick the rat race for so long?

'I have this pleasant glow of achievement when I catch sight of my diploma in its smart red frame. Yes, it was worth it, every minute and every penny.'

CHECKLIST

1. **Studying**: do you have somewhere quiet to study? How will you organise your time?

2. **Stamina**: have you got what it takes to complete the whole course? Can you cope with the pressure of exams?

3. **Support**: do you have close friends and family to help you if the going gets tough? Will your enthusiasm carry you through?

4. **Qualifying**: can you visualise yourself as a fully fledged practitioner with your diploma on the wall of your treatment room?

6

Setting Up in Practice

FINDING PREMISES

The environment you work in will be an important factor in the success of your practice. If it is warm, bright and welcoming, it will be a place where you and your clients can relax and feel at ease. It needs to be smart and convey the right kind of professional image, clinical yet with plenty of homely touches such as plants and pictures. The entrance should be attractive and inviting. The waiting room should be comfortable with up-to-date magazines available. Your treatment room should be quiet, decorated in calming colours, an oasis where clients can escape from their hectic lives for a while.

There are several options for the newly qualified practitioner:

- working from home
- renting a room in a centre with other complementary therapists
- renting a room in another business or professional setting.

The option chosen will depend on individual preferences and circumstances. Let's look at each in detail.

Working from home

You may consider this if you have a suitable spare room, if your house is easily accessible and if your family circumstances allow. Be careful to check your lease if you own a flat or if you are in rented accommodation. Some leases specifically ban the use of the premises for business purposes. Contravening this may invalidate your insurance policies. Using part of your own home for business purposes may mean that you become liable for capital gains tax on a proportion of the proceeds when you sell the property. Do take professional advice before you begin.

Advantages of working from home
- It is usually the cheapest option. You will be able to offset some of your household expenses against tax.

- You can always find something to do if a client does not show up, e.g. studying, paperwork or even the washing!

- You have greater flexibility in scheduling appointments.

Disadvantages of working from home
- It can be difficult to separate your personal and your professional life. You might begin to feel that you are always at work.

- You may feel isolated unless you make the effort to network with other practitioners.

- It might be more difficult to create the necessary professional environment amidst the family clutter.

Note: Never see a new client of the opposite sex when you are alone in your own home. For safety's sake, ask a friend or family member to stay in the house. Ensure the client realises that you are not alone.

Working in a centre

Most towns now have at least two or three complementary health centres. These have usually been set up by enterprising people who are passionately enthusiastic about complementary therapies. They provide attractive, well-organised premises for a variety of therapists. They are usually fairly central and easily accessible by public transport. Many have become well established and have a good reputation in their areas. New practitioners will almost certainly be interviewed to make sure they are properly qualified and that they will fit in with the existing team.

Advantages of working in a centre
- You will be able to take part in open days, mailshots and other publicity initiatives organised by the centre.

- The environment is professional, with reception facilities and cleaning provided.

- You are part of a team, with access to support and advice from colleagues.

Disadvantages of working in a centre
- Room rental is payable, even when clients don't turn up and when you are on holiday. However, some centres help new practitioners by offering reduced rents or hourly rental for an initial period.

- Renting a room by the day or half day limits flexibility of appointment times.

- There might be some practitioner rivalry or competition for clients.

Renting your own premises

There are many other settings in which a complementary therapist can prosper. Retail environments are worth investigating, e.g. a room above a hairdresser's might suit a massage therapist or an aromatherapist. A healthfood shop might provide the ideal environment for a homoeopath, herbalist or nutritional therapist.

Therapists who specialise in sports injuries will naturally be drawn to sports and leisure centres, fitness and health clubs, and will probably find a steady stream of clients.

Many towns have business centres where small businesses rent accommodation with shared facilities. You could work alongside accountants, architects and other professionals, sharing reception and other facilities. Check out local dental and chiropody practices too. Such established surgeries may provide excellent premises for complementary practitioners and result in cross-referral of clients.

Advantages of renting your own premises
- Offers independence and separates home and business.

- Brings you in contact with the wider community and may help attract more clients.

- If you work elsewhere for part of the week, you could sub-let your room to another therapist on the days you're not there.

Disadvantages of renting your own premises
- You need to have confidence in your own business abilities.

- It can be expensive (business rates, etc.). Seek professional advice before you start.

- You will probably be required to sign a lease or commit yourself to a specific period. Again, seek advice.

VISITING YOUR CLIENTS

If you wish to avoid the whole issue of finding premises, then consider having a visiting practice. For this you will need to have your own reliable transport and your equipment must be portable. It can be a feasible option for some therapies, particularly massage, aromatherapy and reflexology.

A good sense of humour is essential for coping with challenges such as unruly children, cats who want to sit on the treatment table and clients who live on the 12th floor!

Home visits are ideal for elderly and disabled clients who are unable to travel. It is well worth approaching residential homes in your area. Many homes and day centres are now employing therapists to visit for a day or half day each week.

Business people often prefer to pay extra for a visit rather than spend time coming to you. Some employers, particularly in large cities, are aware that complementary therapies can help combat stress in the workplace. 'On-site' massage therapists are finding work in office blocks, hotels and even motorway service stations.

Organising your visits

- Remember that visiting takes longer, especially in urban areas where traffic jams will affect your punctuality. Invest in a mobile phone so that you can contact clients while you are on the road.

- Make sure you know exactly where you are going and where you will be able to park.

- Arrange to see two or more clients at the same location whenever possible. Plan visits in the same area on the same day.

- Don't try to cover too large an area. Refer people from outside your area to colleagues who live nearer.

- Have a checklist for your equipment. There's nothing more embarrassing than arriving at a client's minus your oils, acupuncture needles or whatever!

Life is never dull for the visiting therapist. Indeed, it can sometimes become too hectic. You might decide to compromise by spending part of your week out in the community and the remainder in your treatment room. This makes for a varied and interesting working week.

Note: Do not agree to a home visit for a member of the opposite sex unless you know that their partner will be there. Tell your family or a friend where you are going and when you expect to be back.

PLANNING YOUR BUSINESS

The typical complementary therapist has a wealth of clinical knowledge and a wonderful, caring nature. He or she will be able to discuss in great depth the merits of various therapies or remedies. However, the very mention of cash flows and profit and loss accounts will have them reaching for the Rescue Remedy! Fortunately, there is no shortage of people willing and able to give professional advice. Before embarking on your new venture you will want to consult the following advisers:

- **an accountant**, for guidance on becoming self-employed, setting up your accounting records, tax-deductible expenses and dealing with the Inland Revenue

- **bank manager or financial adviser**, for information on loans, start-up finance and pension schemes

- **small business advisory centre**, for information on workshops and courses on marketing, bookkeeping, information technology and business planning.

Most complementary medicine training courses now include modules on setting up your own practice. Unless you already have a business background, you will benefit from taking advice from people who know local business conditions. Your teachers might have had much experience of working in London, which will not be relevant if you plan to work in rural Wales.

EARNING A LIVING

Building a career in complementary medicine takes time. The general consensus is that it takes about three years for a practice to become established. In the meantime, the therapist has to eat! You will need to be resourceful to succeed. There are various ways of approaching the problem:

- Continue with your current employment, taking therapy

appointments in the evenings and at weekends. Eventually you will reach the point where you can make your job part-time, if your employment conditions permit. Keep your vision of becoming a full-time therapist as a long-term goal.

- Look for a part-time job, possibly in a related field e.g. in a healthfood store, dividing your week between your job and your practice.

- If you already have a well-paid profession or skill, you may wish to continue with this. One teacher of the Alexander Technique has successfully combined his teaching with thatching for many years.

You will need to think long and hard before giving up the security of a regular pay cheque to become a full-time self-employed therapist. One advantage of working in complementary medicine is that clients generally pay immediately after their treatment. Other types of small business often fail because customers delay payment of invoices, causing cash flow problems.

Setting your fees

Before deciding what to charge, you will need to find out about the going rate for your therapy in your area. Remember that money is a token of appreciation for your services and do not undervalue yourself. As a newly qualified practitioner, you will charge less than those who have many years experience, but don't charge too little. Currently, the rate for complementary therapies is anything from £15 to £30 per hour, depending on the therapy, the skill and experience of the therapist and the area.

Most complementary therapists recognise that people who need their services most are often those least able to pay. Reductions are usually offered for the unemployed, pensioners, students and children.

Working in complementary medicine is often very demanding. Be careful not to overestimate the hours you will work when making cash flow forecasts. This is especially important for bodyworkers who risk repetitive strain injuries to their hands, wrists and arms through overwork.

Dealing with cancellations

This is a problem which will inevitably occur. Clients sometimes cancel because of illness or unforeseen circumstances. There will always be the odd person who completely forgets an appointment. It is usual to charge a proportion of the fee if appointments are cancelled with less than 24 hours notice. It is important to make your clients aware of this.

Bookkeeping

It is imperative to train yourself to keep good financial records from the very beginning. This is crucial for your peace of mind. You will not be an effective practitioner if your books are in a muddle and the Inland Revenue want your self-assessment form tomorrow! Missing the deadline for your tax forms can incur heavy penalties, as can submitting incorrect or incomplete figures.

Set up your books following your accountant's guidelines, using either a manual or computerised system. Make a point of recording what comes in and what goes out each day. If you really can't manage to do this every day, then discipline yourself to set aside an hour each week for accounts. Keep all receipts and invoices relating to purchases for your business and carefully file all your bank documents. The self-assessment regulations oblige you to keep records for five years. An effective filing system is a must.

It is essential to keep a daily record of fees received, items purchased for the business, motoring expenses and business mileage.

Investing in equipment

Ask yourself these questions before buying any equipment for your practice:

1. Is it really essential?

2. Who is the best supplier?

3. Can I afford it?

That swish massage table made in the USA will impress clients and colleagues, but a more basic second-hand model will be perfectly adequate until the money starts to roll in. If money is not a problem, then you can confidently invest in the table knowing that it will give you many years of good service.

Professional journals are usually a good source of information on equipment. Practitioners who are upgrading or retiring will often advertise their surplus items in the classified columns of their association's journal. Suppliers of equipment such as massage tables often take stands at alternative medicine exhibitions such as the Mind, Body, Spirit Festival in London. There are sometimes special deals for orders taken or items bought at such venues.

Your training school may have discount arrangements with certain suppliers. It is worth doing some thorough research before making major purchases. Make sure you are getting both quality and value for money.

To computerise or not to computerise?

An important question. A decent computer, software and printer will cost around £1,000 new. If you are on a tight budget, it might be best to spend this sum on other equipment and delay buying a computer until you are sure you need one. A simple manual record system is perfectly adequate when starting out.

Many complementary therapists consider computers an essential tool. Computerised **Materia Medica** have revolutionised homoeopathic practice, for example, making the selection of remedies much quicker. The growth of the **Internet** means that more and more information will be instantly available to therapists of all disciplines. Internet access is especially important for therapists interested in research. Most **suppliers** of equipment, essential oils, etc. have web sites which can save time when ordering.

Accounts packages make light work of bookkeeping. Some sophisticated packages will even calculate your tax for you. **Publicity material** such as posters and leaflets can be produced quickly and cheaply using desk-top publishing packages. All complementary therapists need to think seriously about developing computer skills if they do not already have them.

CASE STUDIES

Louise sets up shop

Louise jumped at the chance to take over the pretty little shop in the local arcade. The previous owner had sold aromatherapy oils and products, but without specialist knowledge her business had failed. As a recently qualified aromatherapist and reflexologist, Louise saw how the product range could be developed and the adjacent room turned into an attractive treatment room. She explored her ideas with a friend who helped her to write a business plan. The bank advanced a modest loan and Louise took the plunge.

Eighteen months later, she was well satisfied with her progress.

The shop was open every morning from Tuesday to Saturday. Louise stocked a lovely range of oils, toiletries, books, scented candles and burners made by a potter in Cornwall. She had a steady stream of customers, especially around Christmas time when people bought gift vouchers and toiletries for presents. Many customers went on to become massage clients. Louise made a point of chatting to casual browsers, introducing them to the idea of complementary medicine.

In the afternoons she took appointments in the treatment room. She offered sessions to suit everybody, from full aromatherapy treatments lasting an hour and a half to a 20-minute foot massage. Her clients recommended her to their friends. The practice gradually grew and Louise decided that it was time to look for new premises in the High Street.

William creates the right environment

William had always had a passion for hypnotherapy and he was determined to make his career in this field. When he obtained his diploma, he decided to practise from home. This meant converting one of the bedrooms.

William, a keen and competent DIY enthusiast, set out to create a calm and relaxing atmosphere using pastel shades and natural textures. Pale greens, beige and the occasional splash of warm peach, with a few carefully chosen plants, wallhangings and paintings. A comfortable sofa, a reclining chair and a low table and the room was ready.

One of his first clients, Karen, was a massage therapist. 'This room has a wonderful feeling,' she commented at the end of the session. 'It really does help you to relax. Would you take a look at my treatment room and see how it could be improved?' William agreed and created a very soothing, sophisticated environment for Karen to work in. Her clients loved it and she found that her business began to increase.

After this success, William decided to divide his week between seeing hypnotherapy clients and transforming therapy rooms for other practitioners and clinics. 'It makes sense to use all my talents to make a living,' he said. 'And I enjoy the contrast between the relaxed pace of hypnotherapy and the physical work of decorating. I'm about to start training as a Feng Shui practitioner, which will give me another string to my bow.'

CHECKLIST

1. Can you visualise where you would like to set up in practice? Where would you be happiest? Working alone or with others? Town or country?

2. What sort of premises do you envisage working in? What possibilities exist in your area? Would you be able to work from home?

3. What sort of clients would you prefer to work with? Wealthy or disadvantaged? Young or elderly? Could you cope with the mentally ill or physically disabled?

4. Will you be able to survive financially until your practice takes off? Can you take other part-time work for a while? What about start-up finance? How do your nearest and dearest feel about possible insecurity?

7

Promoting Your Practice

DESIGNING PROMOTIONAL MATERIAL

The first step in promoting your practice is to let potential clients know that you exist. Business cards and leaflets can be an excellent way to get your name and therapy known. You will find such cards and leaflets produced by local therapists in health food stores, sports centres, gyms, libraries, community centres and the like. Start by collecting a few and examining them carefully. Which are the most effective and why? This is one way of clarifying your ideas about what might work for you. Factors to consider are:

Cost

How much can you afford to spend on publicity material? You might decide to start with a basic business card and have a leaflet done later.

Design

Do you want to use a particular logo? Is there a symbol or image that says something about you and the way you work? A massage therapist might choose a line drawing of a hand, a practitioner of Chinese medicine might go for the black and white Yin Yang symbol. A graphic designer would be able to produce a sharp, professional logo to reflect the image you wish to project. You might prefer to use the logo of your professional association, if it has one.

Colour

There is no doubt that the use of colour will help your card or leaflet stand out on a noticeboard. Coloured ink on white paper or card or black ink on a coloured background? The permutations are endless and give you the opportunity to create something unique and distinctive. Be guided by your intuition, a good printer and your budget.

How **NOT** to advertise

Ken Kirby and Fran Felman
invite you to the Open Day at
THE COMPLIMENTARY THERAPY CLINIC
Sat 2nd Sept
11.00am – 4.00pm
TALKS • DEMONSTRATIONS • REFRESHMENTS

14 Melrose Mews, Wickmansford WH1 2TN
Tel: 01231 456784

Aromatherapy • Homoeopathy • Reflexology • Reiki

Ken and Fran have bought an expensive box ad in their local newspaper. Are they giving free treatments or do they pay every client a compliment? If they can't even spell 'complementary', would *you* go to them for a treatment?

Fig. 6. Watch for spelling errors in publicity material.

Content

Business cards and leaflets should show your name, therapy, practice address and telephone number. Leaflets need to be carefully written in clear, concise language. Avoid the use of jargon and also that classic spelling mistake, *complimentary* instead of *complementary* (see Figure 6).

Whatever you do, **do not claim that you are able to cure anything**. It is against the law to make such claims, so restrict yourself to saying that your treatment 'may be beneficial for' or 'is often helpful for' certain conditions.

Some therapists include details of their **fees** in their leaflets, others prefer to give this information when clients ring to enquire or book. If you are having a large quantity of leaflets printed which will last for a long time, it makes sense to omit your prices. This way you will not be faced with the task of amending every one by hand if your prices change.

Distributing your leaflets

A well-designed leaflet can serve as a first introduction to clients. It is a way of letting people know something about your background, your training, the therapy you practise and your own unique approach to your work. The next step is to distribute your leaflets around the neighbourhood so that they can be picked up by potential clients. You might also consider doing a mailshot to individuals, businesses and local organisations, hospitals and GPs.

ADVERTISING

Advertising any form of complementary therapy has to be done very carefully. There are restrictions on the claims that can be made about the effectiveness of treatments, as mentioned above. Your professional association may have guidelines on advertising. Check your code of ethics first, and consult the association if you need advice.

A very basic ad in the classified section of your local newspaper is one way of letting the public know that you are open for business. Market researchers have proved that people need repeated exposure to advertising, so you might consider running your ad daily for one or two weeks, or weekly for a month. The ad should give your name, qualifications, therapy and telephone number, with the practice address unless you are working from home and do not wish to encourage casual callers.

Best places to advertise

Advertising in the local press can be very effective for some practitioners. The parish magazine, adult education guide, the local theatre programmes, community newsheets and the like can provide inexpensive publicity. However, once you have advertised in one publication, expect to have a stream of phone calls from advertising salespeople wanting to sell you space in other publications.

Do try to be around when your ad appears. All being well, you will receive some interested enquiries and make some bookings. If you do not have a receptionist to answer in a professional and informed way, then it is better to answer enquiries yourself. If you cannot be there, make sure the answerphone has a friendly, concise message, and reply promptly to any messages left.

Caution is called for

A word of warning to aromatherapists and massage therapists. Despite all the hard work done by genuine therapists to raise the standing of massage therapy in the eyes of the public, the seedy image created by so-called 'massage parlours' remains. Any ad for massage or aromatherapy, however professional, is likely to bring replies from people looking for sexual services. Unless you are based at a reputable centre with a receptionist and colleagues, you would probably do well to forget this kind of publicity altogether.

Yellow Pages

If you can afford it, a listing in *Yellow Pages* and also *Thompson's Directory* is well worth trying. The most cost-effective way of doing this is to get together with other therapists who belong to your professional association and take out a block ad with them. If this is not possible, then a simple line ad will do.

Monitoring your advertising

Keep a record of how many clients you get from different sources. How many saw your ad, how many saw your leaflet (and where?), how many came via the *Yellow Pages*? This information will enable you to decide which forms of advertising are worthwhile and which are not.

Word of mouth

This is by far the most effective form of advertising. Clients who are pleased with your service, who value your skill and expertise and with whom you have built up a good working relationship, will have no hesitation in recommending you to others. As you become more established, you will find that more of your clients come to you by this route than any other. In the early stages of setting up your practice, it is important to ask your clients to recommend you. Don't be afraid to do this, otherwise they might assume that you are already busy and not think to spread the word. Most people will be only too glad to help you get off the ground by giving your cards and leaflets to friends and colleagues with a word of recommendation.

USING THE MEDIA

If you are an outgoing, confident type of person, then call your local newspaper and discuss the possibility of doing an interview or writing an article for them. This can be a really good way of getting clients – and it is free. It will be easier to do this if you have an 'angle', e.g. 'Acupuncturist needles rugby players' or 'Old bakery becomes herbal clinic'.

Keep an eye out for health-related items in the national and local news. As a therapist, you have every right to comment and in doing so, you could generate some excellent publicity, e.g. an aromatherapist might respond to an article about an epidemic of head lice in local schools by writing a letter about the effectiveness of essential oils for this condition. Acupuncturists and hypnotherapists can write about how helpful their therapies can be for people wanting to quit smoking on Non-smoking Day. Seize such opportunities whenever you can.

Radio
Local radio is usually quite accessible and often very effective for complementary practitioners. All stations have some sort of 'chat show' where five- or ten-minute interviews or longer phone-ins are a feature. Listen to your local stations carefully and get to know the presenters before making your approach. One Devon massage therapist gave a radio presenter a massage, answering questions as she worked. It was announced as 'the first naked radio interview' – a phrase guaranteed to grab the listeners' attention.

Some local radio stations already have a weekly 'complementary medicine spot' featuring local practitioners. If this is the case, it will be more difficult for you to get a look in. Even so, listen to these programmes if you get the chance. They might spark off ideas for you, or provide information about local contacts.

Planning and preparation
Any kind of contact with the media needs some planning. Your comments must be clear and concise and arguments carefully thought out. Facts and figures must be checked and double-checked to avoid embarrassing errors. The media, especially radio, is all about spontaneous communication. You could well be faced with questions you cannot answer, in which case it is best to admit your lack of knowledge rather than bluff. On the other hand, an interview can be a great opportunity to educate the general public and find new clients. Don't forget to tell listeners when and where you can be contacted.

GIVING TALKS AND PRESENTATIONS

There are lots of organisations just crying out for speakers on interesting topics. Your local library is probably the best place to go to compile a list of organisations to approach. Good ones to target are:

- Women's Institutes
- ladies circles
- business clubs
- any organisation with which you have personal contact through your leisure or former professional activities.

If you have teaching experience or some previous experience of giving talks, you will have a great advantage when communicating with the public. If you haven't, don't be deterred from having a go. Your enthusiasm and knowledge of your therapy will carry you far, and the necessary skills can be learned. Many adult education centres and small business clubs run courses on presentation skills, and you could well find new clients amongst the course participants. There are also lots of excellent books on public speaking if you do not have access to a course.

Points to consider before giving a talk

- Who will be in the audience? Will they be male or female, or mixed? What is the likely age range?

- Are there topics of particular interest to the group, e.g. business executives and stress, young wives and pregnancy/childhood ailments, the elderly and arthritis, etc. Ask your contact in the organisation for pointers and tailor your talk according to the audience.

- How long will you be required to speak for? Would they like you to do a demonstration?

- What facilities are available at the venue? Will you have access to a flipchart, overhead projector, slide projector?

Preparing your talk

Once you have answers to the above questions, you will be able to plan your talk. It is a good idea to make **notes** on index cards, which are easier to handle than large sheets of paper. Use coloured pens to highlight headings and key words. Whatever you do, don't just read from your notes. This always sounds wooden and is guaranteed to annoy your audience.

It is worth spending some time, perhaps with someone who knows you well, to have a look at your **body language**. If you are nervous when speaking, you might not be aware that you are playing with your pen, continually pushing your spectacles on your nose or whatever. It is equally important to be aware of habitual **speech patterns** too. Phrases like 'sort of' and 'basically' have their place but are often overused.

The first two or three attempts will probably be quite nerve-wracking if you are new to public speaking, but it is certainly possible to have fun giving talks. If you have humorous anecdotes about your therapy, then by all means include them. **Laughter**, along with an easy, relaxed manner and plenty of eye contact, will help you to establish a good rapport with your audience. There are bound to be lots of requests for your **cards** and **leaflets**, so take a good supply with you. If you feel it is appropriate, you could also offer members of the group a **discount** on their first treatment.

DOING VOLUNTARY WORK

After paying an arm and a leg for your training course, you will probably be anxious to start earning some money. However, if you can find two or three hours each week to do some voluntary work, the chances are that you will be richly rewarded in terms of contacts, experience and sheer job satisfaction.

One aromatherapist spent an afternoon a week working in a day centre for long-term psychiatric patients. She did this for a year, during which time her sessions proved to be effective and popular. She approached the management of the centre and asked about the possibility of receiving payment. To her delight, a budget was found and she was paid a respectable hourly rate for the job. Voluntary work can therefore lead to paid employment in some instances.

Working in a centre or institution of some kind can give you access to people suffering from a condition which interests you, e.g. learning disabilities, arthritis in the elderly, cerebral palsy, mental illness. It can be an excellent opportunity to find out how complementary therapies can help these and other conditions. Such work can become the subject of worthwhile research projects for which funding may be obtained.

Where can you help?

The list of places which welcome complementary therapists is long:

- residential and day centres run by social services and health service trusts, catering for the elderly, disabled, mentally ill
- hospitals and hospices
- schools for children with special needs
- charities, e.g. Age Concern, Mind, Scope.

Your local volunteer bureau will be able to put you in touch with other places in your neighbourhood. Use your own personal contacts if you can, as this is usually the easiest route into any organisation or centre.

Making a difference

By doing voluntary work, you will be helping to improve the quality of life for the clients. You will be helping on both physical and emotional levels. The majority of the people you work with would otherwise be unable to afford any kind of complementary therapy. Voluntary work will also bring great benefits for you as a person and a practitioner. It will give you invaluable experience and broaden your understanding. You may have the opportunity to develop expertise in a particular area.

The paid staff with whom you work may not have had any experience of complementary therapies. Some may be downright sceptical. This could present you with a challenging situation which you will need to handle with tact and diplomacy. On the other hand, the staff who are interested will be able to use you as a resource to increase their own knowledge. Some might even become paying clients.

Saying goodbye

All voluntary work must be undertaken with commitment if you, your clients and the organisation are to get the best from it. If you find that your practice is building up fast and you can no longer spare the time, then try to arrange for another therapist to take over, or at least give the centre plenty of notice that you intend to go.

TRADING YOUR TALENTS

In recent years over 400 **Local Exchange Trading Systems** (LETS) have sprung up all over Britain. Members exchange goods and services for a local currency instead of £ Sterling. Every LETS has a directory listing members' offers. Accountancy, DIY, craft work, cleaning, childcare, language tuition, organic produce, desktop publishing, computer skills – your nearest LETS may be able to supply all these and more. Exchanging your therapy skills for services you need will obviously save your hard-earned cash.

Your local library should be able to tell you if there is already a LETS in your area. Joining is a simple matter of completing an application form listing your offers and your requests. There is usually a small membership fee to pay. Your details will appear in the next directory or newsletter and you will be sent a book of credit slips, which you write out like cheques, but in local currency. Trading can begin immediately. You do not have to earn local currency before you can spend.

Self-employed therapists need to keep a record of LETS earnings because these should be declared for tax purposes. However, any LETS units spent on the business, e.g. for accountancy, motor repairs, graphic design, etc., may be offset against tax. Tax, of course has to be paid in sterling, but it is accepted in LETS that self-employed members charge a proportion in £s to cover this and also to pay for any materials used, e.g. oils, herbs, etc.

Most LETS have social events of some kind and are a great way of making new friends. Plugging into this network can provide lots of good contacts amongst community-minded people. You will also meet other therapists who will be able to treat you if the need arises.

CASE STUDIES

Nil desperandum

David replaced the receiver thoughtfully. Joan really should be home by now. He knew she was going to a meeting this evening. He was concerned about his friend, and decided to pop round to check she was alright. He hadn't spoken to her for days and didn't feel he could leave another answerphone message.

Joan was in her dressing gown and obviously not her usual sunny self. The flat was untidy and the washing up had not been done for days. 'This isn't like you, Joan,' said David. 'Are you ill?' 'I've been really low for a few days, can't seem to find any energy,' replied

Joan, and burst into tears. David put the kettle on and Joan confided that she was deeply disappointed about her career. She had spent thousands of pounds training in aromatherapy and herbal medicine and had recently given up her full-time job in order to concentrate on her practice.

'I've given talks, my leaflets are scattered over the whole town, I've spent hundreds on advertising, and from all that there have been ten enquiries. Ten in four weeks. And only four actual bookings. Why did I bother? How am I going to pay the rent if this continues?' She sank into the deep sofa and reached for more paper hankies. 'I can't even be bothered to mix myself some herbs for the depression. Oh, I'm so angry with everything.'

'It sounds to me as though you're trying too hard and expecting too much too soon. You won't be in a fit state to see anybody if you carry on like this,' said David. 'Look, why don't you book an appointment with Emily and talk things over with her? She didn't get her business going overnight, I'm sure.' He passed Joan a big mug of milky tea.

'Now, I've got two more suggestions,' he continued. 'One, how about offering new clients a free 20-minute consultation? Two, how about coming to the Picture House with me – there's a brilliant new comedy film starting in half an hour.'

'David – you're a real friend! Excuse me while I get dressed,' said Joan as she disappeared into the bedroom. 'Free 20-minute consultations...? Yes, definitely worth a try! Who's in the film?'

Trevor drums up trade

Trevor was just beginning to become established as a sports masseur in Leeds when his wife's firm offered her a promotion to their office in Manchester. He was overjoyed to see Ellie so happy. She deserved this new job and he could easily fit his working life around hers for a couple of years. He decided that he would carry on working at the sports centre in Leeds on Mondays and Tuesdays, spending a couple of nights with friends. The rest of the week would be spent in Manchester, making contacts and getting to know the area.

Trevor and Ellie joined the LETS, trading their skills for 'bobbins' instead of £s. They made several friends, including Bob, who invited Trevor to talk at the leisure centre where he worked. The manager offered Trevor the use of a small room at the centre. Within a couple of weeks, the business cards and leaflets were circulating and clients began to come along. Never backward in coming forward, Trevor made a point of asking every client to recommend him as he was new to the area and was just getting his business off the ground. He gave each of them several cards and asked them to put the cards on the noticeboards where they worked. Most people were only too happy to help. Adverts in the local papers drew a few more clients.

The first three months were very slow. Instead of sitting around worrying, Trevor would walk around the centre and chat to people. Occasionally if someone was particularly interested, he would offer a free 15-minute foot massage as a 'taster'. Gradually the business built up until Trevor had two full days a week at the centre. He continued to travel across the Pennines to Leeds each week and enjoyed the feeling of being consistently busy.

CHECKLIST

1. What sort of professional image do you wish to promote? Can you reflect your chosen image in your business stationery?

2. Make a list of places to advertise. Give yourself a budget and decide on your strategy.

3. Practise giving a talk on your therapy to your nearest and dearest. Build up your confidence to go public.

4. Consider doing some voluntary work locally. This will give you a foothold in the community, along with some very good practical experience.

5. Keep your enthusiasm flowing and believe in yourself.

8

Consolidating Your Practice

BUILDING A REPUTATION

It takes time to build a good reputation. The essential elements of a good reputation include the following:

Clinical competence, judgement and skills

These factors will determine your effectiveness as a practitioner. You must be able to put together all the different strands of your training so that you can deliver the very best treatment for each individual client. As a newly qualified therapist, the information from your course will be fresh in your mind. However, getting your diploma is just like getting your driving licence. It isn't until you are out on the road on your own that you really master the art of driving. Likewise, it isn't until you are in your treatment room with your own clients, making your own decisions and seeing the results of those decisions, that you really start to develop as a practitioner.

The more clients you see and successfully treat, the more your clinical competence, judgement and skills will improve. This brings with it extra confidence, which will enable you to get a real 'buzz' from your work.

Continued learning

It is important to build on your initial training by attending advanced courses whenever you can. Don't be in too much of a hurry to do this. Allow a year or so to fully digest and assimilate your training, then investigate the possibilities. There is a wealth of **postgraduate courses** in most disciplines, which will enable you to specialise in certain aspects of your therapy and add to your knowledge in a systematic way.

Every discipline of complementary medicine is growing at a rapid pace. This means that therapists have to work hard to keep abreast of new developments in their fields. It is also advisable to subscribe to one or two professional **journals** and give yourself time to study them.

Attending conferences

Many professional associations hold annual conferences. These are an excellent source of contacts and new knowledge. They can be expensive, but are usually held in attractive venues such as university campuses, and make a welcome weekend break for the busy therapist. The conference organised every two years by the International Journal of Aromatherapy, for example, includes a dazzling variety of seminars and workshops presented by experts in the field.

The people you meet at such events can become firm friends over the years. Ideas sparked off in such a stimulating environment can encourage you to explore different areas of your work. Above all, attending a good conference will fill you with fresh enthusiasm. This growing expertise and confidence will all help to enhance your reputation. Allow years rather than months for this to happen. It is a gradual process which cannot be hurried.

Professional manner and quality of service

Your training school will have given you much guidance on the correct way to approach clients, how to take an effective case history and how to build a good rapport. It is usually wise to stick to these established methods which have been tried and tested by teachers who have had successful practices, at least when you start out. As your confidence increases, you will naturally evolve your own style and begin to do things in ways that suit you, whilst still adhering to basic principles.

Dressing the part

How you dress will depend very much on the therapy you practise. For therapies like massage, aromatherapy and herbalism where there is a risk of spilling oils and liquids on clothing, it is practical to wear a white coat or overall. Nowadays it is possible to find workwear which is both fashionable and smart if you don't want to look too clinical – try suppliers of clothing for dental surgeries and beauty therapists. (Remember that such specialist clothing is a tax-deductible expense.)

If you decide to abandon the whole idea of wearing a white coat in favour of something less clinical, for instance, then do ensure that you choose a style of dress that is still in keeping with professional standards. Clients will inevitably judge you by first impressions. Older people in particular are likely to be critical of wacky clothing, whereas you could quite happily dress in a flamboyant way if working with students. It is up to you to decide what sort of working image you wish to project.

Being there for your clients

The quality of the service you provide in terms of appointment scheduling, reliability and follow-up care will all count towards your reputation. If you often need to change appointments, double-book yourself, and flit from clinic to clinic, never staying anywhere very long, then you will have little chance of building up a reputation. Your clients must know where to contact you if they need advice, reassurance or help, and you need to make yourself available for them.

Many therapists find that the best way of doing this is to have a regular phone-in time for their clients, say 1–2pm or 6–7pm on weekdays. In this way, you are giving people access to you without encroaching into your private time.

Getting feedback

It is sometimes disheartening for therapists to receive no feedback from clients. If you wish to know whether your treatments have been successful and also keep in touch with particular clients, ask if you can ring them a couple of weeks after their last appointment. Most people will appreciate your concern.

CO-OPERATING WITH COLLEAGUES

As you become established in your area, make every effort to network with other therapists and to learn more about their therapies. The best way to do this is to have treatments from them. This way you gain personal experience of how different therapies work. It will sometimes be necessary to refer clients on, so you will need a good pool of contacts in various disciplines.

It is always tempting to think that your therapy is the best thing since sliced bread, and that you are the best thing that ever happened to your therapy. Cast these delusions of grandeur aside. Cultivate a bit of humility and insight so that you can recognise when a client is no longer benefiting from seeing you and when another therapy, or a more experienced therapist in your own discipline, is to be recommended. You simply do not have the right to waste a client's time or money. In the long run, they will respect you for your honesty.

A few examples

1. Massage therapist Margaret has been seeing client Emily for several months. The effects of her treatment last for some days, then Emily's neck and shoulder muscles tighten up again. Emily is tall and lean, walks with a stoop and spends long hours at a word-processor. Margaret recommends a course of lessons in the Alexander Technique which will enable Emily to correct the postural causes of her pain.

2. During a course of treatments for back pain, Sam confides that he is having marital problems. Osteopath Phil explains that emotional tension can often exacerbate physical problems, and recommends that Sam considers having some counselling alongside the osteopathy.

3. Acupuncturist Elaine has been treating Martin for knee pain for a few weeks, with some improvement. However, she knows that the problem will not be resolved unless Martin loses a lot of weight. With as much tact as she can muster, she refers him to a nutritional therapist.

Knowing when not to treat

It is of course *vitally* important that all complementary therapists should be able to spot the signs of serious disease so that they can refer clients to medical doctors. Besides learning when to treat, every therapist needs to know when *not* to treat. This should be covered in some depth in your training course.

CASE STUDY

Liam develops his expertise

After obtaining his licentiate in acupuncture, Liam rented a room in a local natural health centre. The acupuncturist there, Julia, had more work than she could cope with, so new enquiries were passed on to Liam. Both practitioners had trained at the same college and so had much in common. They formed a good working relationship and made a point of meeting regularly to discuss various aspects of their work. Their combined energy and enthusiasm earned them many recommendations.

Liam's client list grew longer and he discovered that he worked particularly well with elderly clients. He approached a local nursing home and began to hold weekly clinics there. He took several postgraduate courses relevant to this work and eventually became something of an expert on acupuncture for the elderly. This led him to write articles for a professional journal and he also decided to set up a research project with funding from a local charitable trust.

'I've always enjoyed the company of older people and acupuncture certainly improves the quality of life for many of them,' said Liam. 'Painful conditions like arthritis and rheumatism can often be alleviated and energy levels often improve too. The work is immensely satisfying and I do seem to have built something of a reputation in this area, which gives me the feeling of being established in my career. It's taken ten years but I can honestly say I'm pleased with the way things have worked out.'

WORKING WITHIN THE NHS

Opportunities for working in GP practices, hospitals, hospices and other health service establishments are increasing rapidly. Some NHS trusts now have staff with responsibilities for introducing complementary therapies into clinical settings.

Will there ever come a day when complementary therapies are to be found in every hospital and health centre as a matter of course? Let's hope so.

Finding an opening

Finding work within the NHS is undoubtedly easier for therapists who already have a medical background. If you have trained in the NHS then you will understand the protocols and procedures. You will also understand the language and terminology. Most important of all, you will have the contacts.

Therapists without a medical background who wish to find opportunities in the NHS need to network as much as possible. It is a case of following up whatever local leads you can find in the areas of work which interest you. Stay alert to the possibility of finding an opening as a volunteer. You might be able to find funding when the project has become established.

Working in a bureaucracy

The NHS trusts are official bodies which have to operate within strict rules and regulations. As a complementary therapist working in this environment you will be bound by the same rules, in addition to the code of ethics for your own therapy. Under the terms of your contract, you will be obliged to respect patient confidentiality at all times. Any records you are asked to keep will have to be stored according to official guidelines. You may be required to attend compulsory courses for such topics as fire safety and infection control.

You should make a point of understanding the staffing structure of the department where you are employed. You may be asked to liaise with one particular member of staff who has responsibility for overseeing your work. Attendance at meetings may also be necessary. Prepare yourself well and make the most of your opportunity to build bridges between orthodox and complementary medicine.

Where are the therapists in the NHS?

In recent years, many doors have opened for therapists in various parts of the UK. Massage and aromatherapy are most in demand, though other therapies are also gaining entry.

1. Gita is a nurse who has trained in **aromatherapy**. She has a part-time post in a **hospice** where she supervises a team of volunteer therapists. She is responsible for scheduling the treatments and the therapists' rota, training the therapists in the principles of palliative care, maintaining the stocks of oils and liaising with doctors.

2. One of Sara's clients was a secretary at a **large regional hospital**. She thought it would be beneficial for her colleagues to have massage and spoke to her boss. Sara now has two afternoon sessions at the hospital as part of the **stress management programme** for staff. She offers **back massage** or **reflexology sessions**. Staff are allowed one half-hour session per month.

3. Simon worked as a doctor for five years before training in **acupuncture**. He now practises in a special **clinic for pain control** in a teaching hospital. He is also studying hypnotherapy and hopes to introduce this into the clinic soon. The next step will be a research project on complementary approaches to pain control.

4. Arthur thought his career in the **ambulance service** had ended when he suffered a back injury. He recovered with the help of **massage therapy**, and decided to become a therapist himself. He

persuaded his employers to let him treat injured colleagues. The three-month trial was so successful that Arthur is now employed full time. He works in different locations in a purpose-built ambulance. Other ambulance services are about to introduce similar services.

COPING WHEN THE GOING GETS TOUGH

Life as a complementary therapist is not always a bed of roses. This is fine. This is how it should be. Lolling on a bed of roses will make you lazy and complacent. The occasional challenge will sharpen your wits and keep you on your toes. What challenges are you likely to encounter?

Professional challenges

You have just got your practice nicely established. It is growing at just the right pace and you feel that you have 'arrived'. Then along come two therapists in the same discipline and they set up in a smart new clinic down the road. They decide to launch their practice by offering half-price treatments for the first six weeks.

Don't panic. Go and see them. Have a treatment from them. Can you learn anything from them? Maybe you need to spruce up your premises, smarten your image? Spice up your marketing? Your visit reveals that they are better qualified than you are, though you have several more years experience. You realise that you are becoming set in your ways, so you enrol for that postgraduate course you meant to do last year.

You will almost certainly encounter challenges of one kind or another. Use them to calmly assess your strengths and weaknesses. Many challenges will turn out to be blessings in disguise, encouraging you to make changes and preventing you from becoming stale.

Personal challenges

Your personal life should ideally be supportive and nourishing. Sometimes it will be, sometimes it won't. No matter how stable your present set-up is, it will inevitably change. The changes may throw you off balance and your emotions could well go haywire. If you are particularly well-grounded and controlled, you may be able to cope without your clients suspecting a thing. Most therapists are only human, however, and will be more accustomed to sorting out clients' problems than their own.

If you find yourself in difficulties, the first thing to do is to admit it. The next thing to do is to cancel your appointments and give yourself some time off. Arrange for a colleague to act as a locum if necessary. Then get help if you need it. This may be some treatment from a colleague, counselling or perhaps a retreat in the country. Your clients probably will not desert you, in fact you will probably be surprised at how supportive some of them will be. They will definitely not expect you to carry on seeing them despite your bereavement, illness or whatever. They are human too and they will understand.

Remember to treat yourself as you would treat a client who is going through the same trauma. You owe it to yourself and your clients to give yourself the best possible care. And remember too that any crisis is an opportunity for personal growth. You will develop strength and experience which will eventually put you in a better position to help clients who suffer in similar ways.

CASE STUDY

Amanda and Jim take a break

Amanda and Jim met at chiropractic college. They married and set up a joint practice. The practice grew and they decided to expand it into a clinic with a herbalist, a homoeopath and an aromatherapist. The clinic became known as a centre of excellence locally. Close links were forged with the local hospital and a research project on complementary approaches to arthritis was set up. The results were published and other hospitals became interested. The clinic's reputation grew, and so did the pressure of work for Amanda and Jim.

After nine years, it was clear that their relationship was in difficulties. If these could not be resolved, then the clinic would soon be in difficulties too. 'Frankly, we were both exhausted,' admitted Amanda. 'We had given everything we had to our clients, the clinic and the research project. We simply had nothing left for each other.'

They decided that it was time to reassess their own personal needs and take a complete break. A sabbatical year in Canada and the USA seemed the ideal solution. They corresponded with chiropractic associations and received information about conferences, workshops and seminars. They planned their holiday of a lifetime, interspersed with conferences and meetings along the way.

Amanda and Jim drafted in two experienced chiropractors to take their places while they were away. The sabbatical was a great success. When they returned home, strengthened and refreshed, they decided to start another research project sparked off by their American studies. The clinic had done well in their absence and their locums were sorry to leave. Amanda and Jim looked forward to getting back into the swing of things. Their trip had renewed their faith in their work and in each other.

'We had been in a rut for a long time without realising what was happening,' said Jim. 'The trip gave us a chance to relax and take stock of our lives. It was good to have time to be together without the pressure of work. It has taught us how important it is to balance work and play. We'll make sure we take more breaks in future. The trip was a marvellous experience. We grew tremendously, both personally and professionally.'

CHECKLIST

1. Do you have a realistic idea of how long it will take you to establish your practice? Have you spoken to other therapists about their experiences?

2. Can you set and maintain high standards of organisation, punctuality and reliability in your practice?

3. Are you prepared to continue your professional education by taking postgraduate courses, reading the journals and attending conferences?

4. How do you plan to take care of yourself? What steps will you take to keep yourself in good physical, mental and emotional health?

9

Long-term Planning

There are few established career structures in complementary medicine. It is up to each practitioner to decide where his or her interests lie, and to carve out a career accordingly. Some practitioners are happy to spend their whole life working with one therapy, furthering their knowledge by attending advanced courses and gradually becoming experts in their field. Others find that they are inspired to explore different therapies and different approaches. Some are drawn to teaching or research. Let's look at the possibilities.

ADDING MORE STRINGS TO YOUR BOW

After practising for some time, many therapists realise that their treatments would be more effective if they had extra skills. This often leads to the study of a whole new therapy. Therapists usually branch out into areas which complement what they already do, e.g. massage and reflexology, kinesiology and nutritional therapy, healing and aromatherapy. However, it sometimes happens that a therapist enters a totally different field from the one he or she first trained in, leading to another complete career change.

It is not uncommon for ambitious therapists to do two major trainings, e.g. acupuncture and Chinese herbal medicine, or osteopathy and homoeopathy. One exceptionally talented lady combined yoga teaching, Alexander Technique, osteopathy and acupuncture. She had a very busy practice and obtained first class results with her clients. This suited her very well for some years, then she realised that her social life no longer existed. An extended holiday redressed the balance.

Advantages of adding more therapies
- Additional diagnostic approaches enable you to get to the root of the problem more quickly.

- Additional techniques make treatments more effective.

- More rapid and longer-lasting improvement for clients.

- Ability to work with a wider range of clients.

- More variety in your work.

- You will meet new colleagues in your training.

Disadvantages of adding more therapies
- Requires additional financial investment.

- Requires investment of time and energy.

- Danger of too much knowledge resulting in less clarity.

- Need to join another professional association and pay for an additional insurance policy.

There are endless combinations of therapies. You can devise your own unique combination which will make your approach different from that of any other therapist. Just make sure that you don't get carried away and try to add too many therapies too soon. You would run the risk of becoming Jack of all trades and master of none. It is always wise to consolidate your knowledge in one area before moving on to another.

CASE STUDIES

Gabi branches out into health kinesiology
Gabi had a diploma in nutritional therapy and had been in practice for four years. She was generally happy with her career and was starting to get quite busy. She noticed that she was beginning to attract clients with more varied problems, many stemming from emotionally traumatic events in the past. Gabi had done some basic training in kinesiology and used this to help choose the correct vitamins and supplements for clients.

She had read that kinesiology could be used to help clear past trauma as well as to help balance the body and the mind. Gabi decided to do a full practitioner training in health kinesiology. She found that her new skills helped her to get to the root of clients' difficulties more quickly and she was able to facilitate more rapid healing. The focus of her work changed to reflect her new abilities and brought her even more new clients.

Eric enrols for acupuncture

Eric enjoyed his work as a sports masseur but was aware of the strains it placed on his own body. After seven years in practice he was having some problems with both wrists and elbows. He knew that he wanted to continue working in complementary medicine and so decided to train in acupuncture. This turned out to be an important turning point in his life. He met his wife at the college.

After qualifying, Eric set up a practice specialising in sports medicine. He used massage techniques where necessary, but his main focus was acupuncture. He was delighted with the improvement in his career – and in his personal life.

TEACHING COMPLEMENTARY THERAPIES

Getting a teaching qualification

This is the first step for the therapist who wishes to go into teaching. The City and Guilds Certificate in Further Education Teaching (C&G 7306 or 7307) is the minimum qualification you should aim for. This can be obtained through part-time study, usually one evening or half-day a week for one academic year. Even better is the Cert. Ed. which requires two years, covers the subject in much greater depth and is designed for those who intend to make teaching their main career.

These qualifications give practical skills including:

- lesson planning and timing

- teaching methods, e.g. project work, working in groups

- presentation skills

- use of visual aids, e.g. overhead projectors, flipcharts

- preparation of handouts and course materials

- evaluating and assessing learning.

There will also be tuition in the theory of learning and education policy. In order to enrol on one of these courses, you will need to have some teaching already arranged (a minimum of 6 hours a week is required for the Cert. Ed.). Your tutors will visit you several times during the course to observe you in the classroom.

These courses are offered at colleges in most large towns. The fees are a tax-deductible expense. The courses attract people from all professions, e.g. nursing, catering, building, which makes for an interesting group of students. You will gain a great deal of confidence and encouragement from your tutors and fellow students.

Teaching adult education classes

This is a good starting point for the therapist who has been in practice for a few years and wants to start teaching. Most local education authorities offer a selection of courses in complementary therapies. The ones most commonly taught in evening classes are massage, aromatherapy, reflexology, yoga, homoeopathy, herbalism and shiatsu. Kinesiology is also offered in some areas. Some therapies, e.g. acupuncture, clearly cannot be taught in this way. However, a qualified acupuncturist could offer a class on acupressure or on the philosophy of Chinese medicine.

Designing a course

Adult evening classes are usually recreational and are attended by people who want to learn some practical skills to use with friends and family. Some students use such classes as 'tasters' before deciding whether to go on to qualify professionally. Theory should be kept at a basic level and presented in 'bite-sized chunks', backed up with handouts. You will need to balance theory and practical work carefully, making sure that your approach is not too academic or serious.

Most terms are ten or twelve weeks long, and most classes last for two hours. The autumn term is generally the best attended. People have had their holidays and are ready to learn something new. It is sometimes a struggle to keep the student numbers up in the winter term when the weather is cold, especially in rural areas.

If you wish to offer a ten-week introduction to your therapy, decide just how much information you can reasonably expect to teach in that time. Draw up a course outline and some sample handouts. Enclose these in a folder together with your CV and submit them to the adult education department. If your proposals are approved, you may be invited for interview and placed on the local authority's list of tutors.

Making the class enjoyable

Many students at evening classes will have done a day's work by the time the class begins. You might have had a full day of appointments too. It is vital to keep your classes fairly lighthearted. Playing gentle music during practical sessions is a good way of lightening the mood. Don't try to structure every minute of the class, but give students time to chat amongst themselves and share their own experiences. Many lasting friendships are formed in such settings. You may also find that some of your students become regular clients.

Giving workshops

Many therapists enjoy teaching one-day or weekend workshops. These can be an excellent way of generating publicity for yourself and your therapy. Some therapists have generated quite a following and become well known through their workshops. There is a lot of organisation and hard work involved in this sort of project. Sound business skills are required. You need to ensure that you make a profit after paying for room hire and publicity. Consider teaming up with a colleague to share the load – and the fun.

Essential ingredients for success are:

- an attractive, easily accessible venue

- reasonable price, giving value for money

- well-designed publicity posters

- publicity circulated to right people and places in good time

- workshop well planned and organised

- presentation confident and professional.

If your first efforts meet with success, plan more workshops to follow.

An easier method is to write to groups or institutions which might be interested in your therapy and offer to put on a workshop for them. Schools of Nursing and Occupational Therapy, student unions at local colleges or universities and large companies are worth approaching. If your proposals are accepted, you may be offered both a venue and a group of eager students. You can then tailor your course to suit the needs of the group.

CASE STUDY

A massage course for the Women's Group

Janine was asked to give a course in basic massage to members of the Women's Group at the local university. She put together a series of six evening classes, concentrating on back and face massage. The course was received with great enthusiasm. Some of the students were at a stressful stage in their courses. They were delighted to discover the deep relaxation massage can bring. One student remarked that these were the most useful classes she had taken in her three years at university.

Teaching on established courses and at universities

As complementary medicine becomes more integrated into mainstream health care, the demand for practitioners will increase. The demand for teachers will therefore also increase. There will be plenty of opportunities for practitioners with good clinical experience and teaching skills.

Many colleges welcome back their graduates as clinical tutors or lecturers. This has the advantage that you are teaching in a familiar environment with the people who trained you. You will already be familiar with the philosophy and aims of the college too.

Some therapists are able to teach their special subjects on courses in different therapies, e.g. an acupuncturist teaching point location and the five element theory on a shiatsu course, an osteopath teaching anatomy for a massage college.

One major shiatsu school now offers its own teacher training programme. Other schools may well follow this trend, which would help to raise teaching standards generally in complementary medicine.

As more and more universities offer courses in complementary medicine, the teaching opportunities in this sector will increase. Such opportunities are likely to be relatively well paid. The increasing amount of research will ensure plenty of work in the academic side of complementary medicine. The next few years seem set to bring exciting new initiatives and rapid progress.

Setting up your own school

This is a possibility for experienced therapists who have excellent business and communication skills. A substantial amount of capital is needed to invest in premises and equipment. Such an ambitious venture must be carefully planned down to the last detail. It brings with it heavy responsibilities and the prospect of great achievement and rewards.

There are schools of all sizes within complementary medicine, ranging from the large colleges of acupuncture and osteopathy, with their own premises and a large staff, to very small schools of massage where one main teacher instructs a dozen students at a hired venue. Some schools have charitable status which brings certain administrative advantages. The majority are run as commercial business ventures.

For many years, most training in complementary medicine has

been concentrated in the South of England, creating difficulties for students based in the North. This is now changing, with many more opportunities opening up in the Midlands, the North and in Scotland. There is still a need for schools in many smaller towns.

WRITING ABOUT COMPLEMENTARY THERAPIES

There is an insatiable demand for information on all aspects of complementary medicine. This creates a lot of scope for the practitioner who writes well and wishes to branch out in this direction. Writing often follows on quite naturally from teaching. It demands a disciplined and organised approach, a fertile imagination and the ability to communicate your own enthusiasm to your readers. Help with the technical aspects of writing and advice on getting your work published is available in the wide range of How To Books. The usual advice for any writer is, of course, to write from your own experience.

There are several possibilities for the complementary practitioner turned writer:

Writing for magazines and newspapers

There are many magazines which specialise in health matters, e.g. *Here's Health*, *Men's Health*, *Positive Health*. Some are aimed at therapists and healthcare workers, others are aimed at the general public. Most of the vast range of women's magazines have health pages. National newspapers usually have a section on health which appears weekly. There are plenty of publications to approach, but it is a very competitive market. Getting started is often a question of having the right contacts.

Writing a book about your therapy

There are lots of books on every therapy already, and if you have an original, innovative approach, there's room for yours too. The usual procedure is to get together an outline of chapter headings and sub-sections and submit your proposal to a publisher. If this is accepted, you will be asked to produce a sample chapter. Be realistic when negotiating deadlines – make sure you don't promise too much too soon.

Books may be written for different markets. There seems to be a great demand for introductory books with lots of self-help techniques for the reader to try at home. The demand for books aimed at the experienced therapist will grow steadily as more people qualify and set up in practice. There is certainly a growing market for good academic textbooks in every complementary therapy. One enterprising school of shiatsu has published its own textbook. This is now used by schools all over the world and has been translated into several languages.

Writing a book about an aspect of health
Books about complementary approaches to various conditions are always in demand, e.g. asthma, arthritis, cancer, depression, slimming, the menopause. The list is endless. If you have specialised in treating particular disorders in your practice, you may eventually wish to share your knowledge and expertise by writing a book. Your book may be aimed at the general public, or written for therapists, depending on your interests and the depth of your research.

RESEARCHING INTO COMPLEMENTARY MEDICINE
The opportunities for research are unlimited. If complementary medicine and conventional medicine are ever to become fully integrated, then a great deal of research must be carried out in every area. The effectiveness of individual therapies, the effectiveness of various remedies, herbs and supplements, possible changes in health policy – there is a need to investigate all these and more.

The universities are emphasising this by including research methodology in their complementary health degree courses. This covers such topics as how to write a research proposal, designing a protocol, the use of statistics, questionnaires, evaluation, monitoring results, and ethics. Postgraduate research degrees are now being offered by the universities. The University of Exeter offers MPhil and PhD research degrees at the Centre for Complementary Health Studies, which are generally one year full-time or two years part-time, though some students may take longer.

It is possible to undertake research outside the universities, of course. Many projects up and down the country are being carried out in hospitals and other institutions. Sometimes research is conducted by the professional associations; for example, the International Federation of Aromatherapists carried out research into the effectiveness of aromatherapy treatment for endometriosis, a painful complaint which affects some women.

Funding for research projects may be obtained from some trusts, large companies and charities. One charity, the Foundation for

Integrated Medicine, is currently funding research into reflexology for childhood asthma, homoeopathy for childhood asthma, osteopathy for asthma, Alexander Technique for Parkinson's disease, Marma therapy (Indian massage technique) for stroke victims and diagnostic tests for lower back pain. The Foundation will consider only properly costed proposals which meet the highest scientific standards.

CASE STUDIES

Alice gets to grips with her business

Mike Meredith cast an experienced eye over his daughter's accounts. Alice had given up a well-paid job in the civil service to become a complementary therapist. She had trained in remedial massage, kinesiology and Reiki healing. This was her third year in business and Mike could see that she was struggling. He hadn't wanted to interfere, but when Alice sold her car and replaced it with an old banger, he decided it was time to offer his help. Realising that she needed to take a long, hard look at her career, Alice accepted.

'As I see it, the main problem is that you are not thinking of your work as a business,' said Mike. 'I appreciate that what you are doing is more satisfying than the administrative work you did before, but you are adopting the ostrich approach to your long-term finances. You've paid for these extra courses from your savings, not from income. You haven't sorted out a pension and your standard of living is beginning to drop. You need to be clear about your priorities in life and plan accordingly.'

Mike and Alice spent the evening deep in discussion. The result was a plan which would help Alice adopt a more realistic approach to her business:

- Organise appointments only on three days a week. Alice would devote one day a week to studying and consolidating her knowledge with a view to combining her different skills more efficiently. Another day would be devoted totally to marketing, i.e. arranging talks, distributing her leaflets and cards, writing a newsletter to mail to her clients and local businesses.

- Put up her fees. They had not increased in three years.

- Enrol for a teacher training course at the local college. Put together a course to teach at the adult education institute for the following academic year.

- Investigate the possibilities of working within the NHS.

'Like a lot of therapists, I'm no business person,' said Alice. 'Dad has shown me that I must change my attitude if I want to succeed in the long term. I feel much more confident now I have done some planning.'

The planning and marketing paid off. Eighteen months later, Alice had a waiting list of clients and her income had increased greatly. She was enjoying her teaching and planning to set up a school with a friend the following year.

A successful career in reflexology

Elsa had a very successful reflexology practice in a small market town. She was often asked by her clients if she would consider teaching them the basics so that they could treat family and friends. This led to a series of introductory workshops, which in turn led to an evening class at the college in the next town. Elsa enjoyed teaching so much that she decided to make this her main focus. She gained a teaching qualification and then set about opening her own school.

There was a great deal of work involved in this and Elsa did most of it single-handed. She often stayed up till midnight printing out notes for her students. Most of her teaching was at weekends in a beautiful room at a farm on the edge of town. It was an attractive and peaceful venue where the atmosphere was just right for learning and healing.

Elsa's courses were validated by the British Register for Complementary Medicine, who inspected the school at intervals. Elsa was a perfectionist who insisted on the highest standards, from both her students and herself. Eventually the school needed its own space, so she rented a suite of rooms in a large Georgian building in town. Elsa invited other teachers, one a former student, to join her. Life became more hectic and after ten years, Elsa decided it was time to hand over the school to her associates.

She didn't simply put her feet up. The Register asked her to become one of the school inspection team and she also acted as an external examiner for a school in France. Elsa made sure that she also had time to get down to writing a book about reflexology for women. She had been collecting material for this for years. When she looked back, she was very pleased at the way her career had progressed.

Careers in complementary medicine often unfold naturally from the practitioner's work, with one opportunity leading to another as expertise increases and interests develop. It is a new and exciting field with unlimited possibilities for those who are dedicated and enthusiastic.

Appendix – University Courses in Complementary Medicine

The more academic student wishing to make a full-time career in complementary medicine should consider taking a degree course. Contact the universities for their latest prospectus. A-level or equivalent entry requirements usually apply. Biology/physiology or chemistry A-levels are specified for certain courses. Consult the prospectuses for current details. Mature students may receive accreditation for prior learning. Applications for undergraduate degree courses are usually made through The University and Colleges Admissions Service (UCAS), Fulton House, Jessop Avenue, Cheltenham, Glos. GL50 3HS. Tel: (01242) 227788.

Applications for Diploma and postgraduate courses should be made direct to the university.

NB: Some of the schools of acupuncture, herbal medicine, homoeopathy, nutrition and osteopathy listed in Useful Addresses are now offering qualifications which are validated by universities. Check with the schools for up-to-date details.

University of Central Lancashire
Preston PR1 2HE. Tel: (01772) 201201. Fax: (01772) 892935. Web site: *http://www.uclan.ac.uk*

BSc(Hons) Health Sciences for Complementary Medicine. 3 years full-time. A general course giving an introduction to a range of therapies. Further study is necessary to obtain practitioner status.

BSc(Hons) Herbal Medicine. A 4-year course to be validated by the National Institute of Medical Herbalists. A full practitioner qualification.

BSc(Hons) Homeopathic Medicine. A 4-year course for full practitioner qualification.

University of Durham
Centre for Health Studies, 32 Old Elvet, Durham DH1 1HN. Tel: (0191) 374 1840. Web site: *www.durham.ac.uk*

Offers facilities for postgraduate research degrees in complementary medicine. Applications to: Complementary Medical Association. Tel/fax: (020) 8305 9571. Web site: *www.the-cma.org.uk*

University of Exeter
Centre for Complementary Health Studies, Dept of Lifelong Learning, St Lukes, Heavitree Rd, Exeter EX1 2LU. Tel: (01392) 264498. Fax: (01392) 433828. Email: chs@exeter.ac.uk Web site: *http://www.ex.ac.uk/dll*

MPhil/PhD research degrees in Complementary Health Studies. The Centre for Complementary Health Studies was established in 1987 as the first university centre run by complementary health practitioners. It aims to provide continuing professional development for healthcare professionals, i.e. those already working in orthodox or complementary medicine, or in associated disciplines, who have day-to-day responsibility for patients. Courses are usually 1 year full-time or 2 years part-time, but some may be extended over 4 years.

University of Glamorgan
School of Applied Sciences, Pontypridd CF37 1DL. Tel: (01443) 480480. Fax: (01443) 480558. Web site: *www.glamorgan.ac.uk*

BSc(Hons) Chiropractic. A 4-year full-time course followed by 1 year of further clinical training, plus 1 extra year of supervised clinical practice.

University of Greenwich
Avery Hill Campus, Avery Hill Rd, Eltham, London SE9 2UG. Tel: 0800 005 006 (admissions), (020) 8331 8494 (School of Health Studies). Web site: *www.gre.ac.uk*

BSc(Hons) Complementary Medicine. A 3-year degree course (2 years for students with existing healthcare qualifications). 3 routes offered:

Complementary Therapies, for qualified therapists/healthcare professionals or those with general interest.
Aromatherapy – practitioner training to satisfy requirements of the Aromatherapy Organisations Council.
Stress Management – approved by Complementary Medicine Association and Guild of Complementary Practitioners.

Middlesex University
Queensway, Enfield, Middlesex EN3 4SA. Tel: (020) 8362 5161. Fax: (020) 8362 5463. Web site: *www.mdx.ac.uk*

BSc(Hons) Traditional Chinese Medicine. A 5-year full-time training, with at least 6 months of the final year spent in Beijing.

BSc(Hons) Herbal Medicine. A 3-year course with an optional fourth year to obtain practitioner status. Validated by the National Institute of Medical Herbalists.

BSC(Hons) Osteopathy (in collaboration with The College of Osteopaths). A 5-year part-time course.

Napier University, Edinburgh

Faculty of Health Studies, 74 Canaan Lane, Edinburgh EH9 2TB. Tel: (0131) 536 5678. Web site: www.napier.ac.uk

BSC(Hons) Complementary Therapies (Reflexology)
BSC(Hons) Complementary Therapies (Aromatherapy)

These two degrees are part-time and can be structured to suit individual requirements, up to a maximum of 5 years.

BSc(Hons) Homeopathy. Students are required to be qualified health professionals in nursing, midwifery, health visiting, medicine or pharmacy.

Degree programmes in Acupuncture, Herbal Medicine and Chinese Medicine are planned.

Oxford Brookes University

School of Healthcare, Academic Centre Level 4, John Radcliffe Hospital, Oxford OX3 9DU. Tel: (01865) 221576. Fax: (01865) 220188. Web site: *http://www.brookes.ac.uk*

BA(Hons) Complementary Therapies (Clinical Aromatherapy). 2–3 years full-time course for registered healthcare professionals with at least 6 months post-registration experience. Can be combined with other subjects for Joint Honours degree, e.g. Health Care Studies, Palliative Care, Rehabilitation.

Oxford School of Osteopathy, School of Biological and Molecular Sciences, Gipsy Lane, Oxford OX3 0BP. Tel: (01865) 484100. Fax: (01865) 48417. Web site: *http://www.brookes.ac.uk*

BSc(Hons) Osteopathy and Myotherapy. A 4-year part-time course for practitioner status.

University of Salford

Salford, Greater Manchester M5 4WT. Tel: (0161) 295 5000. Fax: (0161) 295 5999. Web site: *http://www.salford.ac.uk/healthSci/index.htm*

BSc(Hons) Complementary Medicine Practice. A 3-year full-time course. Includes acupuncture, herbal medicine and energy-based bodywork. Application has been made for accreditation with the British Acupuncture Council.

Bsc(Hons) Complementary Medicine and Health Sciences. 3 years full-time. A wide-ranging course which students can tailor to meet their own interests. Students will be able to go on to further study with other colleges to obtain practitioner status. Placements within the Health Service and abroad are a feature of the course.

MSc and Postgraduate Diploma courses are also offered.

University of Surrey
European Institute of Health and Medical Sciences, Guildford, Surrey GU2 5XH. Tel: (01483) 876740. Web site: *http://www.eihms.surrey.ac.uk/*

MSc/Postgraduate Diploma in Chiropractic. An intensive 7-semester course which leads to full professional qualification in 2 years and 4 months. Students must have a BSc in a biomedical subject or a qualification as a healthcare professional with sufficient background knowledge in biomedical subjects.

Thames Valley University
Wolfson Institute of Health Sciences, 32–34 Uxbridge Rd, Ealing, London W2 2BS. Tel: (020) 8280 5344. Web site: *www.wolfson.tvu.ac.uk*

Diploma in Higher Education in Complementary Medicine. A part-time course taking between 2 and 5 years, designed for health professionals who wish to increase their understanding of complementary medicine and the role it can play in offering patients greater choice in health care (in conjunction with The Letchworth Centre for Homoeopathy).

BSC(Hons) Ayurvedic Medicine. A 3-year course in collaboration with the Ayurvedic Company.

University of Westminster
Centre for Community Care and Primary Health, Cavendish Campus, 115 New Cavendish Street, London W1M 8JS. Tel: (020) 7911 5082. Web site: *www.wmin.ac.uk/cccph/*

BSc(Hons) Health Sciences (Chiropractic)
BSc(Hons) Health Sciences (Complementary Therapies)
BSc(Hons) Health Sciences (Herbal Medicine)
BSc(Hons) Health Sciences (Homoeopathy)
BSc(Hons) Health Sciences (Nutritional Therapy)
BSc(Hons) Health Sciences (Therapeutic Bodywork)

All the above are 3-year full-time courses with long year status, i.e. tuition from September to mid-August, with some modules requiring attendance during holiday periods. The Therapeutic Bodywork course may be taken on a part-time basis over 5 years.

All courses include clinical experience. The CCCPH runs its own community Polyclinic. MSc and Postgraduate courses are also offered.

University of Wolverhampton
School of Health Sciences, 62–68 Lichfield Street, Wolverhampton WV1 1DJ. Tel: (0192) 321000. Web site: *www.wlv.ac.uk*

BSc(Hons) Complementary Therapies. 3 years full-time or up to 6 years part-time. There are 3 routes: Aromatherapy, Reflexology or Generic. The Generic route is designed for those students who already have existing expertise in complementary therapy, so that they can secure an academic qualification to underpin their practice.

Useful Addresses

This list is not exhaustive. There are so many small schools, especially for massage, aromatherapy and reflexology that it would be impossible to list them all. Inclusion or omission is not intended to imply recommendation or criticism. Contact umbrella organisations or professional associations to find courses in your area. Some schools hold courses in several different venues around the country. Many teachers are willing to travel if there is a demand for their services in a particular area, so it is often worth approaching schools direct – you might be able to help set up workshops in your area. Many schools and colleges advertise their courses in the health magazines. The *Positive Health* magazine training directory and website are established as especially popular places to advertise: the magazine is published monthly and the web site address is: http://*www.positivehealth.com*

ACUPUNCTURE

British Acupuncture Council, 63 Jeddo Road, London W12 9HQ. Tel: (020) 8735 0400. Fax: (020) 8735 0404. Email: info@acupuncture.org.uk Web site: *www.acupuncture.org.uk*

The College of Traditional Acupuncture, Tao House, Queensway, Royal Leamington Spa, Warwickshire, CV31 3LZ. Tel: (01926) 422121. Fax: (01926) 888282. Email: info@acupuncture-coll.ac.uk Web site: *http://www.acupuncture-coll.ac.uk*

College of Integrated Chinese Medicine, 19 Castle Street, Reading, Berks RG1 7SB. Tel: (0118) 950 8880. Fax: (0118) 950 8890.
Email: admin@cicm.org.uk Web site: *www.cicm.org.uk*

The International College of Oriental Medicine, Green Hedges Ave, East Grinstead, West Sussex RH19 1DZ. Tel: (01342) 313107. Fax: (01342) 318302 Web site: *www.orientalmed.ac.uk*

The South West College of Oriental Medicine, 35 North View, Westbury Park, Bristol BS6 7PY. Tel/fax: (0117) 907 8891. Email: info@swcom.org.uk Web site: *http://www.swcom.org.uk*

The London College of Traditional Acupuncture and Oriental Medicine, HR House, 447 High Road, London N12 0AZ. Tel: (020) 8371 0820. Fax: (020) 8371 0830. Email: pathways@lcta.com Web site: *www.lcta.com*

School of Five Element Acupuncture, 13 Mandela Street, London NW1

ODU. Tel: (020) 7383 5553. Fax: (020) 7383 5503.
Email: sofea@clara.co.uk Web site: *www.sofea.co.uk*
Northern College of Acupuncture, 163 Holgate Road, York YO24 4DF. Tel: (01904) 785120. Fax: (01904) 780386. Email: info@chinese-medicine.co.uk Web site: *www.chinese-medicine.co.uk*

ALEXANDER TECHNIQUE

The Society of Teachers of Alexander Technique (STAT), 20 London House, 266 Fulham Road, London SW10 9EL. Tel: (020) 7351 0828. Fax: (020) 7352 1556. Email: enquiries@stat.org.uk Web site: *www.stat.org.uk* (Umbrella organisation.)
Professional Association of Alexander Teachers, 20 High Street, Norton, Stockton-on-Tees, TS20 1DN. Tel: (01642) 363542. Email: Cta1226987 @aol.com Web site: *www.paat.org.uk*
Cumbria Centre for Alexander Teacher Training, Fellside Centre, Low Fellside, Kendal, Cumbria LA9 4NJ. Tel: (01539) 733045. Fax: (01539) 724684. Email: enquiries@fellside.f9.co.uk Web site: *www.fellside.f9.co.uk*
Hampstead Alexander Centre, 4 Marty's Yard, Hampstead High Street, London NW3 1QW. Tel: (020) 7435 4940. Fax: (020) 7794 2652. Email: robinsimmons@btinternet.com Web site: *www.alexanderteacher.free-online.co.uk*
North London Teachers' Training Course, 10 Elmcroft Avenue, London NW11 0RR. Tel: (020) 8455 3938. Email: jmagidov@btclick.com
Bristol Alexander Technique Training School Association, 37 Bellevue Crescent, Bristol BS8 4TF. Tel/fax: (0117) 987 2989. Email: ali.burrows@onet.co.uk
Headington Alexander Training School, 10 York Road, Headington, Oxford, OX3 8NW. Tel: (01865) 765511. Fax: (01865) 454112. Email: S.C@btinternet.com

AROMATHERAPY

Aromatherapy Organisations Council, PO Box 19834, London SE25 6WF. Tel: (020) 8251 7912. Fax: (020) 8251 7942. Web site: *www.aromatherapy-uk.org* (Umbrella organisation representing 12 associations and societies.)
International Federation of Aromatherapists, 182 Chiswick High Road, London W4 1PP. Tel: (020) 8742 2605. Fax: (020) 8742 2606. Email: i.f.a@ic24.net Web site: *www.int-fed-aromatherapy.co.uk*
International Society of Professional Aromatherapists, ISPA House, 82 Ashby Road, Hinckley, Leicestershire LE10 1SN. Tel: (01455) 637987. Fax: (01455) 890956. Email: lisabrown@ispa.demon.co.uk
Register of Qualified Aromatherapists, PO Box 3431, Danbury, Chelmsford, Essex CM3 4HA. Tel: 01245 227957. Fax: 01245 222152. Email: admin@

rqa-uk.org Web site: *www.rqa-uk.org*

The Institute of Traditional Herbal Medicine and Aromatherapy, 12 Prentices Lane, Woodbridge, Suffolk IP12 4LF. Tel: (01394) 388386. Fax: (01394) 388209. Email: info@aromatherapy-studies.com Web site: *www.aromatherapy-studies.com*

Tisserand Institute, 65 Church Road, Hove, East Sussex BN3 2BD. Tel: (01273) 206640. Fax: (01273) 329811. Email: training@tisserand.com

Shirley Price International College of Aromatherapy, Essentia House, Upper Bond Street, Hinckley, Leicestershire LE10 1RS (including aromatology). Tel: (01455) 633231. Fax: (01455) 615054. Email: shirleypricearoma@ compuserve.com Web site: *www.shirleyprice.co.uk*

Scottish School of Professional Aromatherapy and Palliative Training Resources, Albany St, Dunfermline KY12 0QZ. Tel: (01383) 732195. Fax: (01383) 726640.

Scottish Massage Schools, 24 Ellon Road, Bridge of Don, Aberdeen AB23 8BX. Tel: (01224) 822956. Email: smto@isb.co.uk Web site: *scotmass.co. uk*

AYURVEDA

Ayurvedic Company of Great Britain, 81 Wimpole St, London W1M 7DB. (See also Thames Valley University.) Tel: (020) 7224 6070.

The College of Ayurveda (UK), 20 Annes Grove, Great Linford, Milton Keynes MK14 5DR. Tel: (01908) 664518. Fax: (01908) 698371. Email: mauroof@ayurvedacollege.co.uk Web site: *www.ayurvedacollege.co.uk*

BATES METHOD

Bates Method Vision Education & Bates Assn. of Great Britain, PO Box 25, Shoreham by Sea BN43 6ZF. Tel: (01273) 422090. Fax: (01273) 279983. Web site: *www.seeing.org*

BOWEN TECHNIQUE

The Bowen Association, 122 High Street, Earl Shilton, Leicester LE9 7LQ. Tel: (01455) 841800. Fax: (01455) 851384. Web site: *www.bowen-technique.co.uk*

The European College of Bowen Studies, 38 Portway, Frome, Somerset BA11 1QU. Tel/fax: (01373) 461873. Email: ecbs@cwcom.net Web site: *www.thebowentechnique.com*

CHIROPRACTIC

The Anglo-European College of Chiropractic, Parkwood Road, Bournemouth, BH5 2DF. Tel: (01202) 436200. Fax: (01202) 436312. Web site: *www.aecc-chiropractic.ac.uk*

The McTimoney Chiropractic College, The Clock House, 22–26 Ock St, Abingdon, Oxon OX14 5SH. Tel: (01235) 523336. Fax: (01235) 523576. Email: chiropractic@mctimoney-college.ac.uk

The Oxford College of Chiropractic, The Old Post Office, Cherry Street, Stratton Audley, nr Bicester, Oxon OX6 9BA. Tel/fax: (01869) 277111. Email: OCC.admin@btinternet.com

COLOUR THERAPY

International Association of Colour, 46 Cottenham Rd, Histon, Cambridge CB4 9ES. Tel: (01223) 563403. Email: michael@kgrevis.freeserve.co.uk

LIGHT, 28 Devonshire Rd, Bognor Regis, W. Sussex PO21 2SY. Tel: (01243) 822089. Email: dorothye.parker@currantbun.com

Aura Soma, Dev Aura, Tetford, Lincs LN9 6QL. Tel: (01507) 533581. Fax: (01507) 533412.

Avatara, Pitt White, Mill Lane, Uplyme, Devon DT7 3TZ. Tel: (01297) 444772. Fax: (01297) 445514.

Hygeia College of Colour Therapy, Brook House, Avening, Tetbury, Glos GL8 8NS. Tel: (01453) 832150.

Iris International, Fairfields House, Jubilee Rd, Totnes, Devon TQ9 5BP. Tel: (01803) 868037. Fax: (01803) 868079. Email: irisint@eclipse.co.uk

The Oracle School of Colour, 9 Wyndale Avenue, Kingsbury, London NW9 9PT. Tel/fax: (020) 8204 7672. Email: pauline@oracleschool.fsnet.co.uk

The Academy of Radiant Colour, The Natural Healing Centre, Auchendinny, Roslin EH25 9QJ. Tel: (01968) 678789. Email: info@radiantcolour.co.uk Web site: *www.radiantcolour.co.uk*

CRANIOSACRAL THERAPY

Craniosacral Therapy Association, Monomark House, 27 Old Gloucester St, London WC1N 3XX. Tel: 07000 784 735. Web site: *http://www.craniosacral.co.uk*

College of Cranio-Sacral Therapy, 9 St George's Mews, Primrose Hill, London NW1 8XE. Tel: (020) 7483 0120.

Institute of Craniosacral Studies, 7 Alwyn Road, Maidenhead, Berks SL6 5EG. Tel: (01628) 776650. Email: admin@craniosacralstudies.co.uk Web site: *www.craniosacral studies.co.uk*

Karuna Institute, Natsworthy Manor, Widecombe-in-the-Moor, nr. Newton Abbot, Devon TQ13 7TR. Tel/fax: (01647) 221457. Web site: *www.craniosacral.co.uk/kiet.htm*

The Upledger Institute UK, 2 Marshall Place, Perth PH2 8AH. Tel: (01738) 444404. Fax: (01738) 442275. Email: mail@upledger.co.uk (Tuition in various locations in Scotland and England.)

CSPT Scotland, St Helen's Adult Training Centre, 7 West Coates, Edinburgh EH12 5JG. Tel: (0131) 667 5455.

CRYSTAL THERAPY

The Affiliation of Crystal Healing Organisations, PO Box 344, Manchester, M60 2EZ. Tel: (01479) 841450. (Umbrella organisation.)

The Institute of Crystal and Gem Therapists, PO Box 6, Exminster, Exeter EX6 8AY. Tel: (01392) 832005. Email: info@greenmantrees.demon.co.uk

Spiritual Venturers Association, 72 Pasture Road, Goole, East Yorks. Tel: (01405) 769119.

Academy of Crystal and Natural Healing, Highland Holistic Clinic and Study Centre, Craig Gowan, Carrbridge, Inverness PH33 3AX. Tel: (01479) 841257. Email: crystalacademyscotland@hotmail.com Web site: *crystals. eu.com*

Vantol College of Crystal Therapy, 11 Heather Close, New Haw, Addlestone, Surrey KT15 3PF. Tel/fax: (01932) 348815. Email: crystalcollege@ crystalcollege.com

FLOWER AND GEM REMEDIES

The Bach Centre, Mount Vernon, Sotwell, Wallingford, Oxon OX10 0PZ. Tel: (01491) 834678. Fax: (01491) 825022.

International Federation for Vibrational Medicine, Middle Piccadilly Healing Centre, Holwell, Sherborne, Dorset DT9 5LW. Tel: (01305) 849379. Web site: *www.vibrationalmedicine.net*

British Flower and Vibrational Essences Association (BFVEA), 8 Willow Glen, Branton, Doncaster, S. Yorks DN3 3JD. Tel: (01302) 530860. Email: info@bfvea.com Web site: *www.bfvea.com*

Mandragora C S, PO Box 6, Exminster EX6 8YE. Tel: (01392) 832005. Email: info@greenmantrees.demon.co.uk Web site: *http://www.greenman essences.com*

The College of Vibrational Medicine, Unity, Rectory Rd, Gissing, Diss, Norfolk IP22 5UX. Tel: (01379) 677869.
Email: information@crystalherbs.com Web site: *crystalherbs.com*

HEALING

National Federation of Spiritual Healers, Old Manor Farm Studio, Sunbury-on-Thames, Middx TW16 6RG. Tel: (01932) 783164. Fax: (01932) 779648.

Email: office@nfsh.org.uk Web site: *http://www.nfsh.org.uk*

Confederation of Healing Organisations, Suite J, Second Floor, The Red and White House, 113 High St, Berkhamsted, Herts HP4 2DJ. Tel/fax: (01442) 870667. Email: cho.healing@virgin.net (Umbrella organisation.)

College of Healing, Runnings Park, Croft Bank, West Malvern, Worcs WR14 4DU. Tel: (01684) 566450. Fax: (01684) 892047.
Email: info@runningspark.freeserve.co.uk
Web site: *http.//runningspark.co.uk*

HERBAL MEDICINE

The International Register of Consultant Herbalists and Homoeopaths, 32 King Edward Road, Swansea SA1 4LL. Tel/fax: (01792) 655886. Email: office@irch.org Web site: *www.irch.org*

National Institute of Medical Herbalists, 56 Longbrook Street, Exeter EX4 6AH. Tel: (01392) 426022. Email: nimh@ukexeter.freeserve. co.uk Web site: *www.btinternet.com/~nimh/*

The College of Phytotherapy (Herbal Medicine), Bucksteep Manor, Bodle Green, nr. Hailsham, East Sussex BN27 4RJ. Tel: (01323) 834800. Fax: (01323) 834801. Email: medherb@pavillion.co.uk Web site: *www.collegeofphytotherapy.com*

University of Central Lancashire, Preston PR1 2HE. Tel: (01772) 201201. Fax: (01772) 894954. Web site: *http://www.uclan.ac.uk*

East West College of Herbalism, Hartswood, Marsh Green, Hartfield, East Sussex TN7 4ET. Tel: (01342) 822312. Fax: (01342) 826347. Email: EWCOLHERB@aol.com

The Scottish School of Herbal Medicine, Unit 22, Six Harmony Row, Glasgow G51 3BA. Tel: (0141) 401 8889. Email: sshm@herbal medicine.org.uk Web site: *www.herbalmedicine.org.uk*

HOMOEOPATHY

NB: The traditional British spelling has 3 'o's. Some organisations and schools are now using the American spelling with 2 'o's.

The Society of Homeopaths, 2 Artizan Road, Northampton NN1 4HU. Tel: (01604) 621400. Fax: (01604) 622622. Email: info@homeopathy-soh.org Web site: *www.homeopathy-soh.org*

Homoeopathic Medical Association, 6 Livingston Road, Gravesend, Kent DA12 5DZ. Tel: (01474) 560336. Fax: (01474) 327431. Email: info@the-hma.org Web site: *www.the-hma.org*

LCCH Colleges of Classical Homoeopathy, Hahneman House, 32 Welbeck St, London W1M 7PG. Tel: (020) 7487 4322. Web site: *www.lcch.com* (Tuition in London and Preston.)

College of Homoeopathy, address and tel. as above. Email: coh@homoeo pathic-education.com

The British School of Homoeopathy, Homelands Cottage, Burrington, Umberleigh, North Devon EX37 9JH. Tel: (01769) 520462. Email: homoeopath@bigfoot.com Web site: *www.homoeopathy.co.uk* (Tuition in Birmingham and Bristol.)

The Hahnemann College of Homoeopathy, 164 Ballards Road, Dagenham, Essex RM10 9AB. Tel/fax: (020) 8984 9240. (Tuition in London and Birmingham.)

The London School of Classical Homoeopathy, 94 Green Dragon Lane, Winchmore Hill, London N21 2NJ. Tel/fax: (020) 8360 8757.

The College of Practical Homoeopathy, 760 High Road, North Finchley, London N12 9QH. Tel: (020) 8445 6123. Fax: (020) 8445 3784. Email: prachom@this.is Web site: *http://this.is/homoeopathy*

The School of Homoeopathy. Enquiries to: Homoeopathic Training, Orchard House, Merthyr Road, Llanfoist, Abergavenny NP7 9LN. Tel: (01873) 856872. Fax: (01873) 858962. Email: sgracie@alternative.demon.co.uk Web site: *www.homoeopathyschool.com* Tuition in Devon.

The Southern School of Homoeopathy, 78 Highbury Avenue, Salisbury, Wiltshire SP2 7EY. Tel: (01722) 330739. Email: josephinepalmer@aol.com

The Scottish School of Homoeopathic Medicine, Bruiach, Church Terrace, Newtonmoor, Inverness-shire PH20 1DT. Tel: (01540) 673358. Email: judewh@btclick.com (Courses held at different locations in Scotland.)

HYPNOTHERAPY

The National College of Hypnosis and Psychotherapy, 12 Cross Street, Nelson, Lancashire BB9 7EN. Tel: (01282) 699378. Fax: (01282) 698633. (Courses held in Cheshire, London and Edinburgh.) Email: hypnosis-NCHP@compuserve.com Web site: *http://www.nchp.clarets.co.uk*

London College of Clinical Hypnosis, 15 Connaught Square, London W2 2HG. Tel: (020) 7402 9037 Fax: (020) 7262 1237. (Courses also held in Exeter and Bristol.) Email:lcchl@aol.com Web site: *http//www.lcch.co.uk*

Central England College of Clinical Hypnosis, Abbie House, 20 The Hurst, Moseley, Birmingham B13 ODG. Tel: (0121) 778 6676. Email: CECCH7080@aol.com

IRIDOLOGY

School of Medical Iridology, 12 St. Georges Rd, London NW11 0LR. Tel: (020) 8905 5509.

Guild of Naturopathic Iridologists, 94 Grosvenor Road, London SW1V 3LF. Tel: (020) 7821 0255.

KINESIOLOGY

The Kinesiology Federation, PO Box 17, Woolmer Green, Knebworth SG3 6UF. Tel: (0116) 261 2326. Email: kfadmin@kinesiologyfederation.org Web site: *http://www.kinesiologyfederation.org* (Umbrella organisation.)

The Academy of Systematic Kinesiology, 39 Browns Road, Surbiton, Surrey KT5 8ST. Tel: (020) 8399 3215. Fax: (020) 8390 1010. Email: info@kinesiology.co.uk Web site: *www.kinesiology.co.uk*

Creative Kinesiology, 10 Forest Houses, Bellever, Devon PL20 6TP. Tel: (01822) 880264. Email: dolphin@silvertree.demon.co.uk

Educational Kinesiology (UK) Foundation, 12 Golders Rise, Hendon, London NW4 2HR. Tel: (020) 8202 3141. Fax: (020) 8202 3890. Email: ekuk@mccarrol.dircon.co.uk

Integrated Practitioner Training, 70A Caversham Road, Kentish Town, London NW5 2DS. Tel/fax: (020) 7485 4215. Email: info@integrated-kinesiology.co.uk Web site: *www.integrated-kinesiology.co.uk*

Middle England School of Kinesiology, 81 Lancashire St, Melton Road, Leicester LE4 7AF. Tel: (0116) 266 1962. Fax: (0116) 208 7800. Email: kinesiologyschool@compuserve.com Web site: *www.mesk.org*

Health Kinesiology, Sea View House, Long Rock, Penzance, Cornwall TR20 8JF. Tel: (01736) 719030. Fax: (01736) 719040. Email: jane@healthk.co.uk Web site: *www.healthk.co.uk*

Three-in-One Concepts Kinesiology, 178 Elmer Road, Middleton on Sea, West Sussex, PO22 6JA. Tel: (01243) 583350. Email: 101761,3231@compuserve.com

The Scottish Kinesiology College, Bog Park Road, Musselburgh EH21 6RT. Tel: (0131) 665 9599. Fax: (0131) 665 9577. Email: skc@freenet.co.uk

MASSAGE

The Northern Institute of Massage, 14–16 St. Mary's Place, Bury, Lancashire BL9 0DZ. Tel: (0161) 797 1800. Email: northern@institute1924.freeserve. co.uk Web site: *www.nim56.co.uk* (Tuition in London and Bury.)

The Clare Maxwell Hudson School of Massage, Lower Ground Floor, York Street Chambers, 68/72 York St, London W1H 1DF. Tel: (020) 7724 7198. Web site: *www.cmhmassage.co.uk* (inc. manual lymphatic drainage.)

Lymphatic Drainage International, PO Box 287, 28 Old Brompton Road, South Kensington, London SW7 3SS. Tel: (020) 7602 5636. Email: lizfletcher@cwcom.net

Essentials for Health, Church Lane Chambers, 10–12 Church Lane, London E11 1HG. Tel: (020) 8556 8155. Fax: (020) 8539 3324. Email: enquiries @essentialsforhealth.co.uk Web site: *www.essentialsforhealth.co.uk* (inc. baby massage, massage for pregnancy.)

The School of Complementary Health, 38 South Street, Exeter EX1 1ED. Tel/fax: (01392) 410954. Email: 101650.60@compuserve.com (Also offers 2-

day introduction to research for complementary therapists, with tutors from the University of Exeter.)

The Academy of On-site Massage, Avon Road, Charfield, Wotton Under Edge, Glos GL12 8TT. Tel/fax: (01454) 261900. (Courses held throughout the UK for qualified massage therapists only.) Email: all@onsitemassage.softnet. co.uk Web site: *www.aosm.co.uk*

London Centre of Indian Champissage, 136 Holloway Road, London N7 8DD. Tel: (020) 7609 3590. Fax: (020) 7607 4228. (Indian-style head massage.) Email: mehta@indianchampissage.com Web site: *www.indian champissage.com*

The Massage Training Institute, 90-92 Islington High Street, London N1 8EG. Tel/fax: (020) 7226 5313. (Courses in Bristol, Cardiff, Southend, Norwich, Sheffield.) E-mail: mti@totalise.co.uk Web site: *www.massage training.co.uk*

TouchPro UK Chair Massage Training, 176 Melrose Avenue, London NW2 4JY. Tel: (020) 8450 3366. Fax: (020) 8450 2026. (Courses for qualified massage therapists only.) Email: uk@touchpro.org Web site: *www.touchpro.org*

Scottish Massage Schools, 24 Ellon Road, Bridge of Don, Aberdeen AB23 8BX. (Courses in Aberdeen, Edinburgh, Inverness, Glasgow.) Tel: (01224) 822956. Fax: (01224) 822960. Email: smto@isb.co.uk Web site: *scotmass.co.uk*

Scottish School of Professional Massage and Remedial Studies, Albany Street, Dunfermline KY12 0QZ. Tel: (01383) 732195. Fax: (01383) 726640.

NATUROPATHY

British College of Naturopathy and Osteopathy, Lief House, 3 Sumpter Close, 120–122 Finchley Rd, London NW3 5HR. Tel: (020) 7435 6464. Fax: (020) 7431 3630. Email: bcd@bcno.ac.uk Web site: *htpp://www.bcno.ac.uk*

General Council and Register of Naturopaths, Goswell House, 2 Goswell Road, Street, Somerset BA16 OJG. Tel: (01458) 840072. Fax: (01458) 840075. Email:admin@naturopathy.org.uk Web site: *www.naturopathy. org.uk*

Incorporated Society of Registered Naturopaths, Kingston, The Coach House, 293 Gilmerton Road, Edinburgh EH16 5UQ. Tel: (0131) 664 3435.

NUTRITIONAL THERAPY

Institute for Optimum Nutrition, Blades Court, Deodar Road, London SW15 2NU. Tel: (020) 8877 9993. Fax: (020) 8877 9980. Email: ion@cableinet. co.uk Web site: *www.ion.ac.uk*

Plaskett Nutritional Medicine College, Three Quoins House, Trevallett, Launceston, Cornwall PL15 8SJ. Tel: (01566) 86118. Fax: (01566) 86301.

Email: lgplaskett@aol.com Web site: *www.pnmcollege.com*

The College of Natural Nutrition, 1 Halthaies, Bradninch, nr. Exeter EX5 4LQ. Tel/Fax: (01392) 881091. Email: cnn@globalnet.co.uk

University of Westminster, Campus Office (Centre for Community Care and Primary Health) 115 New Cavendish Street, London W1M 8JS. Tel: (020) 7911 5000. Web site: *www.wmin.ac.uk/cccph/*

OSTEOPATHY

General Osteopathic Council, Osteopathy House, 176 Tower Bridge Road, London SE1 3LU. Tel: (020) 7357 6655. Fax: (020) 7357 0011. Web site: *www.osteopathy.org.uk* (Umbrella organisation.)

NB: Schools marked * are accredited by the General Osteopathic Council. Others are awaiting accreditation.

*British College of Naturopathy and Osteopathy, Lief House, 3 Sumpter Close, 120–122 Finchley Road, London NW3 5HR. Tel: (020) 7435 6464. Fax: (020) 7431 3630. Email: bcd@bcno.org.uk Web site: *http:// www.bcno.org.uk*

*The London School of Osteopathy, 11 Selsdon Way, London E14 9GL. Tel: (020) 7538 5242. Fax: (020) 7515 5285. Email: lso@mcmail.com

*The British School of Osteopathy, 275 Borough High Street, London SE1 1JE. Tel: (020) 7407 0222. Fax: (020) 7839 1098. Email: admin@bso.ac.uk Web site: *http://www.bso.ac.uk*

The College of Osteopaths Educational Trust, 13 Furzehill Road, Borehamwood, Herts WD6 2DG. Tel: (020) 8905 1937. Fax: (020) 8953 0320.

*European School of Osteopathy, Boxley House, The Street, Boxley, Maidstone, Kent ME14 3DZ. Tel: (01622) 671558. Fax: (01622) 662165. Email: eso.m.stone@dm.krinfo.ch Web site: *www.eso.ac.uk*

School of Osteopathic Education Ltd (Bristol) School House, Milton on Stour, Dorset SP8 5DQ. Tel: (07957) 121008. Web site: *www.soed.net*

REFLEXOLOGY

The British Reflexology Association and Bayly School of Reflexology, Monks Orchard, Whitbourne, Worcester WR6 5RB. Tel: (01886) 821207. Fax: (01886) 822017. Email: bra@britreflex.co.uk Web site: *www.britreflex.co. uk* (Courses held in London, Leeds Birmingham, Liverpool and Edinburgh.)

The British School of Reflexology, The Holistic Healing Centre, 92 Sheering Road, Old Harlow, Essex CM17 OJW. Tel: (01279) 429060. Fax: (01279) 445234. Email: bsr@footreflexology.com Web site: *www.footreflexology. com*

Association of Reflexologists, 27 Old Gloucester Street, London WC1V 3XX. Tel: 0870 567 3320 (Schools throughout the UK.) Email:aor@reflexology.org Web site: *www.reflexology.org/aor/*

International Institute of Reflexology, 255 Turleigh, Bradford-on-Avon, Wiltshire BA15 2HG. Tel: (01225) 865899. Email: reflexology_uk @hotmail.com

The Reflexologists' Society, PO Box 5422, Leicester LE2 2YG. Tel: 0870 607 3241.

Northern School of Reflexology, 32 Handsworth Gardens, Armthorpe, Doncaster DN3 3SZ. Tel: (01302) 835457. Email: geordie@4unet.co.uk

Scottish Institute of Reflexology, 4 Eden Road, Ednam, Kelso, Roxburghshire TD5 7QG. Tel/fax: (01573) 226645. Email: thesir@talk21.com Web site: www.scottishreflexology.fsnet.co.uk

REIKI

The Reiki Association, Cornbrook Bridge House, Cornbrook, Clee Hill, Ludlow, Shropshire SY8 3QQ. Tel/fax: (01584) 891197. Tel: (01981) 550829. Email: reikiassoc_office@compuserve.com Web site: *www.reikiassociation.org.uk*

There are a great many Reiki masters offering courses in all areas of the country. Please refer to the above association and magazines for details of courses in your area. (See Further Reading for magazines.)

SHIATSU

The Shiatsu Society, Eastlands Court, St Peters Road, Rugby CV21 3QP. Tel: (01788) 555051. Fax: (01788) 555052. Email: admin@shiatsu.org Web site: *www.shiatsu.org*

British School of Shiatsu-Do, The Shiatsu Place, 97–99 Seven Sisters Road, London N7 7QP. Tel: (020) 7281 1413. Fax: (020) 7281 1413. Email: shiatsu.do@btinternet.com Web site: *www.shiatsuplace.com*

The European Shiatsu School, High Banks, Lockeridge, nr. Marlborough, Wiltshire SN8 4EQ. (Also in London, Devon, Bristol, Manchester, Greece and Spain.) Tel: (01672) 513444. Fax: (01672) 861459. Email: info@shiatsu.org.uk Web site: *www.shiatsu.org.uk*

The Devon School of Shiatsu, The Coach House, Buckyette Farm, Littlehempston, Totnes, Devon TQ9 6ND. Tel/fax: (01803) 762593. Email: info@devonshiatsu.co.uk Web site: *www.devonshiatsu.co.uk*

Zen Shiatsu and Healing Tao Centre, Third Floor, 19–21 Phipp Street, London EC2A 4NP. Tel: 0700 078 1195. Email: enquiries@learn-shiatsu.co.uk Web site: *www.learn-shiatsu.co.uk*

The Ki Kai Shiatsu Centre, 172A Arlington Road, Camden, London NW1. Tel: (020) 8368 9050. Email: love.light@virgin.net Web site:

www.kikai.freeserve.co.uk
The Shiatsu College, Unit 62, Pall Mall Deposit, 126 Barlby Road, London W10 6BL. Tel: (020) 8987 0208. (Also in Brighton, Bristol, Hastings, Norwich, Newcastle and Edinburgh.) Web site: *www.shiatsucollege.co.uk*
The Shiatsu College, 13 Scone Gardens, Edinburgh EH8 7DQ. Tel/Fax: (0131) 661 6052. Email: Shiatsu@ednet.co.uk Web site: *shiatsucollege.co.uk*

T'AI CHI CHUAN

The T'ai Chi Union for Great Britain, 69 Kilpatrick Gardens, Clarkston, Glasgow G76 7RF. Tel: (0141) 638 2946. Fax: (0141) 621 1220. Email: secretary@taichiunion.com Web site: *www.taichiunion.com*

YOGA

Yoga Biomedical Trust, Yoga Therapy Centre, Royal London Homoeopathic Hospital, 60 Great Ormond Street, London WC1 3HR. Tel: (020) 7419 7911/7195. Fax: (020) 7419 7196. Web site: *www.yogatherapy.org*
The Devon School of Yoga, 'Fourways', Stevens Cross, Sidford, Sidmouth, Devon EX10 9QL. Tel: (01395) 512355. Email: duncan@devonyoga.com Web site: *www.devonyoga.com*
The British Wheel of Yoga, 1 Hamilton Place, Boston Road, Sleaford, Lincs. NG34 7ES. Tel: (01529) 306851. Email: office@bwy.org.uk Web site: *www.bwy.org.uk*
Sivananda Yoga Vedanta Centre, 51 Felsham Road, London SW15 1AZ. Tel: (020) 8780 0160. Fax: (020) 8780 0128. Email: siva@dial.pipex.com Web site: *SivanandaYoga.org*
School of Kundalini Yoga, 103 Spitfire Studios, 63 Collier St, London N1 9BE. Tel/fax: (020) 7837 1850. Email: info@skyoga.co.uk Web site: *www.skyoga.co.uk*

ZERO BALANCING

ZBA UK, 10 Victoria Grove, Bridport, Dorset DT6 3AA. Tel: (01308) 420007. Email: zbauk@aol.com Web site: *http://www.zerobalancing.com*

CENTRES OFFERING A RANGE OF THERAPIES

The Raworth Centre, 20–26 South Street, Dorking, Surrey HR4 2HQ. Tel: (01306) 742150. Fax: (01306) 742163. Email: raworthcen@aol.com Web site: *www.raworth.com*

Offers both full and part-time diploma courses in a wide range of therapies, including massage and aromatherapy, reflexology, sports therapy, iridology and nutrition. Many of the qualifications are based on NVQs and are internationally recognised.

The Complementary Therapies College of Wales, 1–2 Williams Court, Trade St, Cardiff CF10 5DQ. Tel: (01222) 238599. Web site: *http://www.therapieswales.co.uk*

Offers courses in aromatherapy, reflexology, sports massage, sports injury therapy, Touch for Health, Reiki, Indian head massage and more.

Fife Natural Therapies, Complementary Training Centre, 234 Crossgates, Fife KY4 8AJ. Tel: (01383) 732195. Fax: (01383) 726640. Email: fnt@dialstart.net

Offers courses in remedial massage, advanced remedial massage, clinical aromatherapy and reflexology.

UMBRELLA ORGANISATIONS FOR COMPLEMENTARY MEDICINE

Institute for Complementary Medicine, PO Box 194 London SE16 7QZ. Tel: (020) 7237 5165. Web site: *www.icmedicine.co.uk* (Also administers British Register of Complementary Practitioners.) The ICM is actively involved in education and research and parliamentary lobbying.

British Complementary Medicine Association, 33 Imperial Square, Cheltenham, Glos GS50 1QZ. Tel: (01242) 519911. Email: info@bcma.co.uk Web site: *www.bcma.co.uk*

British Holistic Medical Association, 59 Lansdowne Place, Hove, East Sussex BN3 1FL. Tel/fax: (01273) 725951. Email: bhma@bhma.org Web site: *www.bhma.org*
The BHMA was formed in 1993 by a group of medical doctors and students. It is a voluntary organisation for professionals and members of the public who want to adopt a more holistic approach in their own life and work. The BHMA aims to support the holistic approach to health through information, conferences, events and publications.

The Complementary Medicine Association, The Meridian, 142a Greenwich High Road, Greenwich, London SE10 8NN. Tel: (020) 8305 9571. Web site: *www.the-cma.org.uk*
The CMA is the largest professional membership body in the world for complementary practitioners, providing insurance and a range of support services. The CMA is committed to furthering education and research.

The Foundation for Integrated Medicine, International House, 59 Compton Road, London N1 2YT. Tel: (020) 7688 1881. Fax: (020) 7688 1882. Email:

enquiries@fimed.org Web site: *www.fimed.org*
A registered charity initiated at the suggestion of His Royal Highness the
Prince of Wales. The Foundation aims to promote scientific research into
complementary medicine, provide education, promote greater awareness
and collaborate with other medical and complementary organisations.

Healthwork UK, 344–354 Gray's Inn Road, London WC1X 8PB. Tel: (020)
7692 5550. Fax: (020) 7692 7070.

The Government appointed National Training Organisation for health
care.

Guild of Complementary Practitioners, Liddell House, Liddell Close,
Finchampstead, Berks RG40 4NS. Tel: (0118) 973 5757. Fax: (0118) 973
5767. Email: info@gcpnet.com Web site: *www.gcpnet.com*

A professional association for qualified practitioners of complementary
medicine, offering insurance and a public referral register.

MARKETING FOR COMPLEMENTARY PRACTITIONERS

One-day courses are offered throughout the UK by:

The Complementary Business Association, c/o Touch Marketing,
The Wessex, 11–13 West Cliff Road, Bournemouth BH2 5EU.
Tel: (01202) 297301/267416.

Glossary

Chakra. There are seven major chakras linked to the glands in the endocrine system. They are energy centres which receive and distribute energy within the physical body. Read the books by Caroline Myss (see Further Reading list) for an excellent explanation of the functions of the chakras in health and disease.

Essential oil. Highly aromatic oils used in aromatherapy. Most essential oils are extracted by a process of distillation. They may be obtained from leaves, flowers, seeds and bark. They are highly concentrated and should generally be used diluted in a vegetable or 'carrier' oil. Essential oils have many therapeutic properties, both for the body and the mind. They tend to work better in combination than singly.

Fascia. The ligaments and membranous sheaths that surround and connect all our organs, bones and muscles. Fascia helps to hold the body together. It is very flexible and influences many body processes and movements. Craniosacral therapists are particularly concerned with releasing any restrictions in fascial tissue.

Holistic. From the Greek word 'holos', which gives us both 'holy' and 'whole'. Caring for the whole person, i.e. body, mind and spirit. Complementary practitioners take a holistic approach by considering a client's entire lifestyle, including diet, exercise, emotions, relationships, occupation.

Marma. Specific points on the body, similar to acupuncture points, which are used in the Indian system of Ayurveda.

Meridians. The pathways which carry energy (qi or chi) throughout the body. There are twelve main pairs of meridians which are connected to organs or body functions, e.g. spleen and stomach meridians. There are also eight extra meridians. The whole network of meridians serves to connect the physical body to the subtle bodies. The acupuncturist inserts needles at specific points along the meridians in order to correct any imbalances.

Pathology. Symptoms such as fatigue, itching, or pain may appear before disease manifests in the body. Pathology is the study of changes in the body which result in disease and abnormalities.

Phytotherapy. Another term for herbal medicine.

Qi. Also 'chi' and 'ki'. Energy, the life force. Qi flows through the meridians in a specific pattern every 24 hours. For a period of 2 hours one organ is dominant, e.g. peak energy for the stomach is 7–9am. When the flow of Qi is upset for any reason, physical symptoms may result.

Subtle anatomy. Invisible layers of energy which surround the body, known as the etheric, emotional, mental, astral, causal, celestial and spiritual bodies. These link with each other and with the physical body. If they become congested, disease or disharmony may result.

Vibrational medicine. Therapies which act on the physical body and the mind by harmonising the subtle anatomy, e.g. crystal healing and flower essences. Homoeopathy and healing also work in this way. Colour, light and sound can be employed in therapeutic ways. The whole field of vibrational medicine is expanding rapidly and will undoubtedly become more important in the future.

Further Reading

Bookshops and libraries have a huge selection of titles on all aspects of complementary medicine. A list of recommended reading will be provided by your course tutors. This list contains information on some of the magazines and journals which are relevant to practising and student complementary therapists. Most professional associations produce journals which are specific to their therapy. Reading the journals is an essential part of a therapist's work, since these present the most up-to-date information. The books chosen for this list mainly contain information about wider issues and ideas underpinning complementary medicine.

MAGAZINES AND JOURNALS

Positive Health, 51 Queen Square, Bristol BS1 4LH. Tel: (0117) 983 8851. Fax: (0117) 908 0097. Web site: *http://www.positivehealth.com*

Caduceus, 38 Russell Terrace, Leamington Spa, Warwickshire CV31 HE. Tel: (01926) 451897. Fax: (01926) 885565. Email: caduceus@oryx.demon.co.uk

Complementary Therapies in Medicine, Harcourt Brace/Churchill Livingstone, Robert Stevenson House, 1–3 Baxter's Place, Leith Walk, Edinburgh EH1 3AF. Tel: (0131) 535 1720. Fax: (0131) 535 1729. Web site: *http://www.churchillmed.com/journal.html*

BOOKS

Radical Healing, Ballentine, R. (Rider Books, 1999)

The Encyclopaedia of Complementary Medicine, Endacott, M. (ed) (Carlton Books, 1996)

Healthy Business, the Natural Practitioner's Guide to Success, Harland, M. and Finn, G. (Hyden House Ltd, 1990)

Why People Don't Heal and How They Can, Myss, C. (Bantam, 1998)

The Anatomy of the Spirit, Myss, C. (Bantam, 1997)

The Greening of Medicine, Pietroni, P. C. (Gollancz, 1990)

The 'Principles' series of books published by Thorsons give further information about many of the therapies in this book.

Index